ALL FOR
EXCELLENCE
IN EDUCATION

9 Steps To Every Child's Inner Splendor

DR. MALICK KOUYATE

BALBOA.PRESS

A DIVISION OF HAY HOUSE

Balboa Press books may be ordered through booksellers or by contacting:

Balboa Press
A Division of Hay House
1663 Liberty Drive
Bloomington, IN 47403
www.balboapress.com
844-682-1282

Because of the dynamic nature of the Internet, any web addresses or links contained in this book may have changed since publication and may no longer be valid. The views expressed in this work are solely those of the author and do not necessarily reflect the views of the publisher, and the publisher hereby disclaims any responsibility for them.

The author of this book does not dispense medical advice or prescribe the use of any technique as a form of treatment for physical, emotional, or medical problems without the advice of a physician, either directly or indirectly. The intent of the author is only to offer information of a general nature to help you in your quest for emotional and spiritual well-being. In the event you use any of the information in this book for yourself, which is your constitutional right, the author and the publisher assume no responsibility for your actions.

Any people depicted in stock imagery provided by Getty Images are models, and such images are being used for illustrative purposes only. Certain stock imagery © Getty Images.

Print information available on the last page.

ISBN: 978-1-9822-5441-4 (sc)
ISBN: 978-1-9822-5442-1 (e)

Balboa Press rev. date: 09/19/2020

CONTENTS

TO THE READERS

Dear readers, *All For Excellence In Education (AFEIE)* is the Panacea or the universal remedy against:

* *the Fear of Life, the Fear of Death, the Empty Center,*
* *all educational failures at all levels,*
* *all man-made tragedies within and across all cultures.*

To *Educate All For Excellence* is to inspire all children in general and all open-minded teens, adolescents and young adults in particular to know why and how to enjoy and share *Oneness* with full *Self-awareness:*

* *oneness with their loved ones and important others,*
* *oneness between their learning and their true calling,*
* *oneness between their knowledge/skills and their dominant talent,*
* *oneness between what they have to do and what they are called to do,*
* *oneness with almost everyone else's true, transcendent, infinite Self.*

All For Excellence In Education (AFEIE) is a two-way teaching-learning road building process: road between the natural and normal but too often too conflicting two:

* *children in every child,*

* *teaching-learning worlds in every teaching-learning environment,*
* *teaching-learning outcomes in every teaching-learning process.*

Dear readers, there is a place, an ineffable place, deep within and all around each and everyone of us where we each and all are divinely, spiritually and psychologically meant to meet and melt down and be *One* with one another without losing our personal-identity.

All For Excellence In Education (AFEIE) is an ever increasing striving to inspire all children in general and all open-minded teens, adolescents and young adults in particular to know why and how to enjoy and share *the powerful life giving and life animating power of the Harmony* between:

* *their life unavoidable Conflicts,*
* *their life's own personal inner Opposites,*
* *their Persona-mask and their true and total Personality.*

MEET DR. MALICK KOUYATE

Thank you so much for trusting me with your time, energy and resources. My name is Malick Kouyate. I am from Guinea, Conakry, West Africa. I am the author of *How To Educate All For Excellence (Trafford Publishing, 2013)* and the co-founder of *All For Excellence In Education (AFEIE)*.

Early on in my life, my parents, like all loving parents, used to tell me that:

* *God, because of His omnipotence, and a baby, because of his innocence, deal both directly with the heart. Therefore, if I smile at a baby who refuses to smile back, mine is not from my heart.*
* *A child is a love letter written by a whole family at the service of the whole community. Therefore, for every step I take and move I make and action I undertake, I must do so with my whole family and community in my heart.*
* *if the whole world stands on this side, stand still on your own side as long as you know that you are right from the bottom of your own heart. Therefore, I need to be true to my own true Self at any cost, even at the cost of being cast out.*

Some of the steps I took and moves I made and actions I undertook did not meet my parents expectations. I have had my lion share of mistakes, fears, failures, lacks and temporary setbacks.

But, what my parents taught me is still ringing, like a bigone musical melody, into the back of my mind. Looking back, I realize that my parents wanted me to know why and how to act, interact and react, ideally at the same, as:

* *a social human being,*
* *an individual human being,*
* *a spiritual being.*

Unfortunately, I left my parents when I was only 16 years old. Upon their agreement, I went away to pursue my schooling.

In sharp contrast to the time tested ways of life, shared values and solid worldviews my parents wanted me to live by, some of my new day-to-day life experiences away from my parents were telling me that:

* *who I know is more important than what I know,*
* *what I have is more important than who I am,*
* *name, fame and fortune are more important than my shared values...*
* *why then should I bother?*

On the one hand, I love my parents with all my heart. I believe, almost religiously, in all what they taught me. To try to defy or deny what they taught me was to try to defy or deny a vital part of me. To me, that was impossible.

On the other hand, the ongoing negative exposures and experiences all around me, once away from my parents, were too obvious to be denied too.

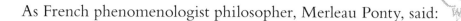

As French phenomenologist philosopher, Merleau Ponty, said:

No one can deny evidence, you have to follow it or to flee from it.

I was very confused. I did not know what to say. I did not know what to do. I did not know which way to go. I was in limbo.

Have you ever been too confused too?

What I love the most...*my honesty, integrity, humility, inner autonomy*...collided with what I hate the most...*hypocrisy, blind conformity...*

What do you do where there is so little or nothing left to do?

It is in the midst of *such a do or die situation* that I started listening more regularly and more attentively to my own small and still inner voice. My inner voice was telling me to hold on tight. My inner voice was telling me to rely on, learn from and build upon *the ineffable something more and bigger and better deep within me and all around me.*

Call it divine love, divine grace, divine guidance... Call it healthy self-love. Call it spiritual love or unconditional love. True and unconditional love has been my first and one of my most *Vital Life Saving Signals* on my long and rocky and slippery road to *All For Excellence In Education (AFEIE).*

Slowly but steadily, I realized that there is a place, an ineffable place, deep within me and all around me where I am divinely, spiritually and psychologically meant to be *One* with full *Self-awareness with:*

* *my loved ones and important others,*
* *my own true, transcendent, infinite Self,*
* *everyone else's true, transcendent, infinite Self.*

I realized that I need to be in touch with and deeply touched by *the Larger than Life* within me and all around me if I am to know why and how to:

* *love truly, forgive, forget, heal, be whole...*
* *live fully alive, enjoy and share a meaningful, peaceful, purposeful life...*
* *be a peaceful culture consumer and become a mindful culture producer.*

But it took me over 48 years of soul searching to be fully aware and deeply convinced that there is a powerful life giving and life animating power by and through which I am meant to be *One* with my own and every else's:

* *true Self,*
* *transcendent Self,*
* *infinite Self.*

Our true, transcendent, infinite *Self* is where we each and all are meant to meet and melt down and be *One* with one another as the same important members of the same important family: *the Human Family.*

At the deepest and/or the highest level, we each and all are divinely, spiritually and psychologically meant to be *One* with one another without losing our personal *Identity.*

DEDICATION

This book is dedicated to my 14 year-old-daughter, Kadiatou Kouyate. You, my dear-other-me, do always remember Pierre Corneille's concern when he said: *"Si jeunesse savait, si vieillesse pouvait."* (*If youth knew, if eldery were able to.*)

A book on *All For Excellence In Education (AFEIE)* is also dedicated to all:

* parents who all are meant to love unconditionally all their children,
* community leaders who all make decisions that impact our daily life,
* children who all need their first educational need for *Belonging,*
* teens who all need their second educational need for relative *Independence,*
* adolescents who all need their third educational need for *Dialogical Encounter,*
* adults who all need their fourth educational need for *Self-navigation.*

Dear parents and community leaders, we adults are all educators to some degree. Whatever we do or whatever we refuse to do may help or may hurt someone close to us including the very innocent *Inner Child* in each and everyone of us all as a whole.

To *Educate All For Excellence* is to inspire all children in general and all open-minded teens, adolescents and young adult in particular to know *why* and *how* to enjoy and share their 4 deepest educational needs for:

* *Belonging,*
* *relative Independence,*
* *Dialogical Encounter between Belonging and Independence,*
* *Self-navigation.*

All For Excellence In Education (AFEIE) is the first and the smoothest road to:

* *active, meaningful and mindful learning,*
* *true and long lasting peaceful culture consumption,*
* *mindful culture production.*

ACKNOWLEDGEMENTS

A book on *All For Excellence In Education (AFEIE)* is an inspiration of all those who believe that we each and all are spiritually meant to meet and melt down and be *One* with one another without losing our personal identity.

All For Excellence In Education (AFEIE) is children' ever increasing striving for *Oneness* with full *self-awareness:*

- ★ *oneness with their loved ones and important others,*
- ★ *oneness between their knowledge/skills and their dominant talent,*
- ★ *oneness between what they have to do and what they are called to do,*
- ★ *oneness with almost everyone else's true, transcendent, infinite Self.*

All For Excellence In Education is children' first and one of their best ways to the best there is:

- ★ *deep within everyone of them,*
- ★ *all around everyone of them,*
- ★ *in between their inner world and their outer world.*

INTRODUCTION

Dear parents and community leaders, *Education,* from its Latin root, *Educare,* means helping someone learn, *grow, develop and prosper including from the Inside Out.*

Indeed, every normal child has virtually:

- ★ *an inner splendor that is in no other,*
- ★ *a priceless inner treasure that is in no other,*
- ★ *a life most favorite love song that has never been sung before.*

All For Excellence In Education (AFEIE) is, in some degree, an Awakening Process of the Inner Splendor buried deep within every normal child.

To *Educate All For Excellence* is to inspire all age appropriate children in general and all open-minded teens, adolescents and young adults in particular to know why and how to:

- ★ *awaken their own personal Inner Splendor that is in no other,*
- ★ *treasure their own priceless Inner Treasure that is in no other,*
- ★ *share their own most favorite love song that has never been sung before.*

Dear parents and community leaders, the smoothest and straightest roads to every normal child's *Inner Splendor* are their 4 deepest *Educational Needs*:

- ★ *for Belonging,*
- ★ *for relative Independence,*
- ★ *for the Magic between Belonging and Independence,*
- ★ *for Self-navigation.*

These 4 deepest *Educational Needs* should be satisfied, ideally, at the same time, if every child is to know why and how to be open and receptive to:

- ★ *the Inner Child and the Outer Child in every child,*
- ★ *the External and the Internal Learning Worlds,*
- ★ *knowledge/skills reproduction and to new knowledge/skills production.*

For instance, children need their External Learning World to Awaken their Internal Learning Word.

They need their Internal Learning World if they are to know why and how to awaken their own *Inner Splendor that is in no other.*

Their Inner Splendor is vital to their will, skills and wisdom to add meaning to their *External Learning World.*

All For Excellence In Education (AFEIE) is a two-way teaching-learning road building process.

The Problem

Dear parents and community leaders, there are two equally important:

- ★ *learners in every child,*
- ★ *teaching-learning worlds in every teaching-learning environment,*
- ★ *teaching-learning outcomes in every teaching-learning process.*

Children' loved ones and important must inspire them to know why and how to:

- ★ be in touch with the two learners in every child,
- ★ learn, at the same time, from their two learning worlds,
- ★ share knowledge reproduction and new knowledge production.

For instance, the natural and normal ongoing *Conflict* between children' first and second deepest educational needs for *Belonging* and for relative *Independence* **is** the first and the deepest root cause of all:

- ★ *educational failures at all levels,*
- ★ *man-made tragedies at all levels,*
- ★ *youth violences within and across all cultures.*

The *Disharmony* between the first and second deepest educational needs for *Belonging* and for relative *Independence* exposes certain teens, adolescents and young adults to what psychologist of

Artistic Creativity, Otto Rank, and depth psychologist and psychoanalyst, Carl G. Jung, call:

* *the Fear of Life, (Otto Rank)*
* *the Fear of Death, (Otto Rank)*
* *the Empty Center. (Carl G. Jung)*

The Fear of Life, the Fear of Death and the Empty Center are the 3 deadliest educational diseases. These 3 deadliest educational diseases are at the root causes of all man-made tragedies, including juvenile delinquency, alcohol, drug, food, sex, opioid addiction...

The Solution

All open-minded teens, adolescents and young adults must know why and how to learn, at the same time, from their two learning worlds if they are know why and how to be open and receptive, ideally at the same time:

* *to their Outer Child and to their Inner Child,*
* *to their External Learning World and to their Internal Learning World,*
* *to their knowledge Reproduction and to their new knowledge Production.*

The world great religious and spiritual traditions and collective wisdom tell us that:

* *we each and all are created at God image,*

- ★ *we each and all are created at God likeness,*
- ★ *God is all loving, all knowing, all powerful.*

For all true believers, that means that we each and all are divinely and spiritually and psychologically meant to be:

- ★ *all loving,*
- ★ *all knowing,*
- ★ *all powerful.*

However, our day-to-day life unavoidable *Conflicts,* our personal inner *Opposites* and our possible fears, failures, lacks and temporary setbacks are also telling us that we each and all are merely:

- ★ *what we know,*
- ★ *what we do,*
- ★ *what we have.*

The larger the gap between who we are divinely and/or spiritually meant to be and who we happen to be in our day-to-day life:

- ★ *the deeper the wound we may inflict to any innocent Inner Child,*
- ★ *the deeper and more unfathomable the possible Inner Void in us,*
- ★ *the more unbearable the possible Pain of our Inner Emptiness.*

When we try to live as if the whole world we live in were merely material, we undermine and compromise our openness and receptivity to:

- ★ *the Larger than Life deep within and all around everyone of us,*
- ★ *ultimate meaning or super-meaning or meaning as divine design,*
- ★ *our strong belief systems, solid worldviews, shared values...*

Without ultimate meaning, solid worldviews, shared values and time tested ways of life, it is impossible for us to face constructively the faceless face of what neurologist, psychiatrist and logo-therapist, Viktor Emil Frankl, calls:

- ★ *the existential vacuum,*
- ★ *the existential frustration,*
- ★ *the frustrated will:*

  1. *to meaning,*
  2. *to power,*
  3. *to money,*
  4. *to pleasure at its lowest level.*

PART I: All For Excellence In Education 3 Founding Blocks

Dear parents and community leaders, All For Excellence In Education (AFEIE) 3 rock solid founding blocks are:

* ★ *the healthy innocent Inner Child in everyone,*
* ★ *the true and long lasting Fulfillment for everyone,*
* ★ *the true and long lasting Inner Peace for everyone.*

PART II: All For Excellence In Education 3 Building Blocks

Dear parents and community leaders, All For Excellence In Education (AFEIE) 3 rock solid building blocks are:

* ★ *the Unity between life unavoidable Conflicts,*
* ★ *the Balance between External Authority and Inner Autonomy,*
* ★ *the Harmony between the pairs of our personal Inner Opposites.*

PART III: All For Excellence In Education 3 Life Giving Powers...

Dear parents and community leaders, All For Excellence In Education (AFEIE) 3 powerful life giving and life animating powers are:

* ★ *peaceful culture consumption,*
* ★ *self-navigation,*
* ★ *mindful culture production.*

PART I

All For Excellence In Education
3 Founding Blocks

Dear parents and community leaders,

All For Excellence In Education (AFEIE)
3 rock solid founding blocks

Or the first *3 Vital Steps* to every normal
Child's Inner Spendor are:

* *the healthy and free and fully alive Inner Child in everyone,*
* *the true and long lasting Fulfillment for everyone,*
* *the true and long lasting Inner Peace for everyone.*

The 3 deepest root causes of all educational failures at all levels

And all man-made tragedies within and across all cultures are:

* *the deeply wounded innocent Inner Child in a child,*
* *the deep and unfathomable possible Inner Void in a child,*
* *the unbearable possible Pain of Inner Emptiness in a child.*

We all know that what will transform education is not another theory, another book, or another formula but educators who are willing to seek a transformed way of being in the world...what we seek is a way of working illuminated with spirit and infused with soul.
(Parker J. Palmer, Ph.D)

CHAPTER 1

Protect the Inner Child

In healing ourselves, we learn that the greatest
wisdom of all lies not in listening to others
but in being true to our deepest selve.
(Lewis M. Andrews, Ph.D)

Dear Teens...Listen to your own
Small and Still Inner Voice

The first rock solid founding block of
All For Excellence In Education
Or the first *Vital Step* to every normal *Child's Inner Splendor*
Is the healthy and free and fully alive
innocent *Inner Child* in every child.
The healthy and free and fully alive
innocent *Inner Child* in every child
Is to *All For Excellence In Education* what
water is to the fish: vital.
Your healthy and free and fully alive innocent *Inner Child*
Is your first step to mental stability,
emotional balance, health growth.
The quality of your life hinges heavily
upon who you are on the inside,
If you are true to your own true *Self,* you
will be true to everyone else.

Dear teens, adolescents and young adults,
There is a place, an ineffable place, deep
within and all around you
Where you each and all are meant to enjoy and share *Oneness:*

★ oneness with your loved ones and important others,
★ oneness between your learning and your true calling,
★ oneness between what you have to do and what you are
   called to do,
★ oneness with almost everyone else's true, *transcendent,*
   infinite Self.

To enjoy and share Oneness with full Self-awareness,
You need first to know why and how to enjoy and share
The will and skills and wisdom you need to cease to be
Who you used to be in order to be
One with the best there is deep within and all around you.

...of all the nostalgia that hunt the human heart,
the greatest of all, to me, is an everlasting longing to
bring what is youngest home to what is oldest in us all.
(Lauren van Der Post, psychoanalyst)

Dear parents and community leaders, the first rock solid founding block of All For Excellence In Education (AFEIE) or the first Vital Step to every normal Child's Inner Splendor is the healthy and free and fully alive innocent Inner Child in every child.

Dear parents and community leaders, depth psychologists and psychoanalysts tell us that there is an innocent *Inner Child:*

* ★ *in every child and every teen,*
* ★ *in every adolescent and every young adult,*
* ★ *in every old man and every old woman of every age.*

The Problem

It is not easy, especially for teens, adolescents and young adults to know why and how to face constructively the faceless face of:

* ★ *their innocent Inner Child elusive existence,*
* ★ *their innocent Inner Child extreme vulnerability,*
* ★ *their innocent Inner Child's deep needs and ultimate longings.*

It is not easy for teens, adolescents and young adults to know why and how to accept, respect, protect, enjoy and share their too elusive, too vulnerable and too demanding innocent *Inner Child.*

Worst, anyone and anything can wound the innocent Inner Child in a child. A wounded innocent Inner Child is like a deadly wounded wild lion. A deadly wounded wild animal can wound anyone or anything close enough starting by itself.

The Solution

Children' loved ones and important others must work harmoniously together to inspire all children in general and all open-minded teens, adolescents and young adults in particular to know why and how to accept and respect and protect:

- ★ *the elusive innocent Inner Child in every child,*
- ★ *the extremely vulnerable innocent Inner Child in every child,*
- ★ *the deep needs of the innocent Inner Child in every child.*

All educators must work together to inspire all open-minded teens, adolescents and young adults to know why and how to:

- ★ *accept their own and each other's innocent Inner Child,*
- ★ *respect their own and each other's innocent Inner Child,*
- ★ *protect their own and each other's innocent Inner Child.*

But it takes true love, strong belief systems, solid worldviews, shared values...to:

- ★ *accept, respect and protect a child you cannot see, touch...*
- ★ *be true to your own true, transcendent, infinite Self,*

- ★ *satisfy your own and each other's Inner Child's deep needs, such as:*
    1. *their honesty, integrity, humility...*
    2. *their subjectivity, originality, vulnerability, infinite possibilities...*
- ★ *their sociability, playfulness, intimacy...*

On the one hand, psychoanalysts tell us that *the Inner Child is the most disowned self in our civilized world.*

On the other hand, they tell us that *the loss of the Inner Child is one of the most profound tragedies in the "growing up" process.* (Hal Stone and Sidarta Winkelman, psychoanalysts)

It is easy to hurt the innocent Inner Child. Loving and caring parents with their own wounded innocent Inner Child may wound their own children' innocent *Inner Child.*

Divine/spiritual love, healthy self-love, unconditional love, faith, divine grace, divine guidance, forgiveness, healing, wholeness, ultimate meaning...is what our children need if they are to be fully aware of:

- ★ *the existence of the innocent Inner Child in every child,*
- ★ *the extreme vulnerability of the innocent Inner Child in every child,*
- ★ *the deep needs of the innocent Inner Child of every child.*

The full awareness of who truly they are deep on the inside is what helps teens, adolescents and young adults to know why and how to change for the better how:

* *they see the world they live in,*
* *they see their our place in the world,*
* *they interact with each other in their day-to-day life.*

Teens, adolescents and young adults must know why and how to be good to their own innocent Inner Child if they are to know why and how to be good to each other's innocent Inner Child.

They need to know why and how accept and respect and protect their own true *Self* if they are to know why and how to accept and respect and protect the Inner Child in everyone else starting by:

* their *loving and caring parents, brothers, sisters...*
* *their inspiring teachers, classmates, coaches, teammates...*
* *their close friends, neighbors, co-workers...*

Be Aware of the innocent Inner Child Elusive Nature

Your innocent Inner Child's existence is not as obvious as the day and the night.

The faceless face of your innocent Inner Child's extreme vulnerability is not easy to face.

Your innocent Inner Child's deep needs and ultimate longings are not easy to satisfy. Your innocent *Inner Child* is, at the same time, the symbol of:

* *the oldest and the youngest part of your true and total Personality,*
* *the strongest and the weakest part of your true and total Personality,*
* *the most intimate and the most disowned part of your true Personality.*

The Problem

In dealing with the innocent *Inner Child*, the dictum is:

There's nothing to say and there's nothing to do.
(Hal Stone and Sidra Winkelman, psychoanalysts)

This is how delicate is the innocent *Inner Child in* us all. This is how difficult it is to deal with the innocent *Inner Child* in us all.

Dear teens, adolescents and young adults, your innocent *Inner Child* can often be deeply wounded by your own:

* *parents, brothers, sisters, friends, foes...*
* *teachers, classmates, coaches, teammates...*
* *self...*

Yet, your healthy and free and fully alive innocent *Inner Child* is vital to your:

* *mental stability,*
* *emotional balance,*
* *healthy growth.*

If you lose, for any reason, your innocent *Inner Child,* you lose so much of the the magic and mystery of your own:

* *growing up process,*
* *healthy self-love, self-esteem, self-confidence...*
* *longing for honesty, integrity, humility, trustworthiness, intimacy...*

The Solution

Be Aware of the innocent Inner Child Extreme Vulnerability

Anyone can hurt the extremely vulnerable innocent *Inner Child* in us all.

Anything can hurt the extremely vulnerable innocent *Inner Child* in us all.

Parents and important others may hurt the innocent *Inner Child of their own children*. Children may hurt their own innocent *Inner Child*. The closer the launching pad, the deeper the wound, as the old saying goes.

The disowned and wounded innocent *Inner Child in a teen, an adolescent or a young adult is* the first and one of the worst root causes of the parenting 3 massive mistakes or:

* *parents'...way as almost the only way,*
* *teens'...way as almost the only way,*
* *parents and their teens with no common way.*

The healthy *innocent Inner Child* determines part of children's ability to:

* *love truly and live fully alive...*
* *forgive, forget, heal, be whole...*
* *enjoy a meaningful life, a peaceful life, a purposeful life, a successful life...*

But, ... *we have not been...able to nurture the needy, vulnerable part of ourselves, we carry around within an angry, sad, childlike residue, which often shapes our adult relationships. (Samuel Osherson, psychoanalyst)*

The *Inner Child's* deep needs and ultimate longings have everything to do with:

* divine love, healthy self-love, spiritual love, unconditional love...
* inner purity, inner peace, inner autonomy, peace with one another...
* honesty, integrity, humility, trust, intimacy, infinite possibilities...

Dear parents and community leaders, our children' *Outer Child* is the child we can see and touch and play with and drop to or pick up from school...

Our children' *Outer Child* is the child who may say *Yes* when he/she means *No* or *No* when he/she means *Yes.*

But our children' innocent *Inner Child* is the exact opposite. Our children' innocent *Inner Child* is the child we cannot see and touch and manipulate...

When healthy and free and fully alive, our children' innocent *Inner Child* is one of their lifelong best friends.

When disowned and wounded and ignored, our children' innocent *Inner Child* is one of their lifelong worst enemies.

As parents and educators, we need to know why and how to parent first our own extremely vulnerable innocent *Inner Child* if we are to know why and how to parent our children' extremely vulnerable innocent *Inner Child.*

As parents and educators, we need to help our children satisfy their educational need for relative *Independence* if they are to know why and how to enjoy and share:

* *their true identity, uniqueness, natural gift...*
* *their inner Peace so vital to their Peace with one another,*
* *their inner autonomy so vital to their self-navigation...*

Dear parents and community leaders,
When only parents win, both parents and children lose,
When only children win, both parents and children lose,
When both parents and children lose, it could be a nightmare
For the whole family, the whole community...
The win-win parenting style is the
first and one of the best ways
To *All For Excellence In Education.*

Our *Inner Child* can often tells us, without any previous experiences or rational explanations:

* *who is who?*
* *who is to be trusted and who is not?*
* *who is likely to hurt us because of their own hurting Inner Child?*

For instance, in falling in love, Mr. Perfect may not escape the intuitive scrutiny of a prospective lover's healthy and free and fully alive innocent Inner Child.

Mr. perfect may have charm and elegance. He may have the knowledge and skills he needs for a well paying job. But any prospective lover with a healthy innocent *Inner Child* may have the intuition to:

* *read between the lines,*
* *see beyond eye can see and to hear what is not said,*
* *discern if Mr. perfect is truly perfect on the Outside and on the Inside.*

The healthy innocent *Inner Child* can also help us move peacefully from:

* *painful relationships such as a hurtful friend or love partener...*
* *situations where there is no hope for healthy growth...*
* *a bossy boss with condescent and demeaning domineering control...*

Who truly we are on the inside, compared to what we know and say and do, is by far the true and best indicator of who truly we are.

7 Vital Life Saving Signal on the Long Road to a *Healthy Inner Child*

As parents and educators, our first rock solid building block of *All For Excellence In Education* or our first *Vital Step* to every normal *Child's Inner Splendor* is the healthy and free and fully alive innocent *Inner Child* in every child.

The 7 *Vital* but too often missing *Life Saving Signals* on the long road to a healthy and free and fully alive innocent *Inner Child* in both parents and their children hinge heavily upon their will and skills and wisdom to know why and how to:

* be open and receptive to the Outer Man and the Inner Man in every man,
* build a two-way teaching-learning road between the 2 learning worlds,
* re-align the teaching-learning to children' innate talent,
* awaken the positive side of the sleeping giant in every child,
* treasure the priceless inner treasure in every child that is in another,
* enjoy the most favorite love song in every child that is in no other,
* share peaceful culture consumption and mindful culture production.

CHAPTER 2

Share the Larger than Life

We sleep with men but rest only when alone
with that something in us greater than us
and larger than life.
(Jalal U. Rumi, mystic poet)

Dear Teens...Be deeply in Touch
with the Larger than Life

The second rock solid founding block
of *All For Excellence In Education*
Or the second *Vital Step* to every normal *Child's Inner Splendor*
Is the *Larger* than *Life* deep within and all around everyone.
Dear teens, adolescents and young adults,
Be in touch with the *Larger* than *Life*
deep within and all around you,
Do it by and through spiritual love, healthy
self love, unconditional love...

Dear teens, adolescents and young adults,
The *Larger than Life* deep within you and all around you
Is your pathway to the wisdom you need to:

* read between the lines,
* learn how to unlearn so that you could learn better,
* see more than eye can see,
* see a message beneath every mess,
* see adversity as a great *university*,
* see a star beyond every scar.

The *Larger than Life* deep within you and all around you
Is your smoothest and straightest and fastest road
To the ineffable divine presence
Or the formless form of the *Absolute* in form
Deep within you and all around you.

One word frees us of all the pain of life.
That word is love.
(Sophocles, a pre-Socratic philosopher)

Dear parents and community leaders, the second rock solid founding block of All For Excellence In Education (AFEIE) or the second Vital Step to every normal Child's Inner Splendor is the Larger than Life:

- ★ *deep within everyone,*
- ★ *all around every everyone,*
- ★ *in between the best there is within and all around everyone.*

All open-minded teens, adolescents and young adults must know why and how to be in touch with and deeply touched by the *Larger* than *Life:*

- ★ *deep within everyone of them,*
- ★ *all around everyone of them,*
- ★ *in between the best there is within and all around everyone of them.*

Open-minded teens, adolescents and young adults need to be deeply convinced that they live in two distinct yet intimately interconnected worlds. They need to know that they live, at the same time, in a material world and in a spiritual world.

The Problem

Certain teens, adolescents and young adults may often try to live as if their whole world were merely material. When they do, they may undermine and compromise their openness and receptivity to:

* *divine love, divine grace, divine guidance...*
* *ultimate meaning or super-meaning or meaning as divine design,*
* *their loved ones and important others' solid worldviews, shared values...*

The Solution

Open-minded teens, adolescents and young adults need to know that the world great religious and spiritual traditions and collective wisdom tell us that *there is always:*

* *something more,*
* *something bigger,*
* *something better.*

What a powerful life giving and life animating power! This is part of what teens, adolescents and young adults need if they are to know why and how to:

* *read between the line,*
* *learn how to unlearn so that they can learn better,*
* *face more constructively their life unavoidable uncertainties.*

Loved ones and important others' solid worldviews, shared values and time tested ways of life are their children' smoothest roads to the *Larger* than *Life:*

* *deep within everyone of them,*
* *all around everyone of them,*
* *in between the best there is within and all around everyone of them.*

True believers know that they each and all are divinely/spiritually meant to be:

* *all loving,*
* *all knowing,*
* *all powerful.*

What a powerful way to face the faceless face of life's natural and normal:

* *unavoidable Conflicts,*
* *personal inner Opposites,*
* *persona-mask and true and total personality.*

Teens, adolescents and young adults' best life is about their ever increasing striving to be, at the same time, their own best:

* *on the outside,*
* *on the inside,*
* *in between their "Inner world" and their "Outer world."*

Open-minded teens, adolescents and young adults need to know that their *Outer World* is, compared to their *Inner World,* what the *Earth* is to the *Solar System,* just a tiny and tinny part of an infinite whole.

For true believers, we each and all are divinely/spiritually meant to know why and how to:

* *love all, including our hurtful friends and foes,*
* *forgive all and forget and heal and be whole,*
* *enjoy and share a meaningful life, peaceful life, purposeful life...*

The Problem

The larger the gap between who our children are divinely/ spiritually meant to be and who they too often happen to be in their day-to-day life, the deeper their already deep *Inner Void*.

When our teens, adolescents and young adults face the faceless face of their possible deep and unfathomable *Inner Void,* no one and nothing material can help them *Fulfill* it:

* *no deep knowledge, no vast practical skills, no well paying jobs...*
* *no food or alcohol or drug addiction...*
* *no name, no fame, no celebrity, no popularity, no cheerful fans...*

The Solution

To *Educate All For Excellence* is to inspire all children in general and all open-minded teens, adolescents and young adults in particular to know why and how to prevent or confront and overcome the possible deep and unfathomable *Inner Void* by and through:

* ⋆ *divine love, divine grace, divine guidance...*
* ⋆ *ultimate meaning or super-meaning or meaning as divine design,*
* ⋆ *divine/spiritual love, unconditional love, forgiveness, healing, wholeness...*

As social human beings with potentialities for spiritually ways of beings, our teens, adolescents and young adults must be slowly aware that they each and all are divinely meant to enjoy and share true and long lasting:

* ⋆ *Fulfillment,*
* ⋆ *Inner Peace*
* ⋆ *Peace with one another.*

They need to be deeply convinced that socially and historically, we all may be totally different from one social group to the other. But psychologically, we each and all are, to some degree, the same important members of the same important family: *the Human Family.*

On their own Words: Persuan poet, Hafiz, asked:
"Would You Think It Odd" if Hafiz says:
I am in love with every church,
And mosque,
And temple,
And every kind of shrine,
Because I know it is in there
That people say the different names
Of the same God."

The Problem

Many people, especially young people, may have hard time knowing why and how to:

- ★ *be in touch with the Larger than Life deep within,*
- ★ *be deeply touched by the Larger than Life all around,*
- ★ *be deeply touched by the Larger than Life within and all around.*

The Solution

Man's deep longing for the *Larger* than *Life* is made obvious in the following life learning and life changing question. The Scriptures ask anyone, with a thinking soul, the following life learning and life changing question:

What do you have when you gain the whole world but lose your own soul?

For all true believers, the obvious answer is *"Nothing."*

How happy it is to be happy, all the time, for no tangible reason! That is one of the great *Secrets* of the world's great seers, sages and saviors.

Their Own Story: Alexander the Great was one of the ancient world's greatest warriors. He conquered and controlled great parts of the ancient world. He had tremendous power over many regions of the world. He had tremendous material possessions.

But one day, Alexander saw a poor philosopher in his poor hut and he asked him, *"Master, what can I do for you?"*

"Go away," answered the philosopher.

On the outside, Alexander has power over almost the whole world. On the other side, Alexander seems to have control over no one including his own self.

Indeed, Alexander died at a relatively young age. He did not die from the swords or the arrows of another great warrior. Alexander died from a sexually transmitted disease.

On the outside, he had dominion over almost the whole world, on the inside, he had control over no one including his own self.

The powerful and the powerless, the rich and the poor...no one seems to be able to enjoy and share true and long lasting meaning in life without:

* *ultimate meaning,*
* *or super-meaning,*
* *or meaning as divine design.*

The *Larger* than *Life* deep within and all around everyone of us is our pathway to true and long lasting *Fulfillment.*

The *Larger* than *Life* within and all around everyone of us is what we need first if we are to enjoy and share true and long lasting:

* *Inner Peace,*
* *Peace with one another,*
* *Peace within and across all cultures.*

But our day-to-day life unavoidable *Conflicts,* our personal inner *Opposites* and our fears, failures, lacks and temporary setbacks are also telling us that we each and all are merely:

* *what we know,*
* *what we do,*
* *what we have.*

The Problem

The world wide spread *Split* between our material world and our spiritual world is dragging so many people, especially young people, into the bottomless abyss of nothingness. Therein, they face the faceless face of what neurologist and logo-therapist, Viktor Emil Frankl, calls:

* ★ *the existential Vacuum,*
* ★ *the existential Frustration,*
* ★ *the frustrated will to meaning, to power, to money, to pleasure.*

The existential vacuum, the existential frustration and the frustrated will to meaning... are 3 major barriers to teens, adolescents and young adults true and long lasting:

* ★ *Fulfillment,*
* ★ *Inner Peace,*
* ★ *Peace with one another.*

The Solution

Transcend the Soma/Spirit/Split

French writer, Michel de Montaigne, said that:

Man is a whole, if you mutilate one part, you destroy the whole.

Like Michel de Montaigne's man, our world is also a whole.

If we *Split* it, we destroy it as the world's great religious and spiritual traditions and collective wisdom tell us it is.

Our world is not merely a material world. Our world is also a spiritual world. When we try to live as if the world were merely material, we face the faceless face of a meaningless and a lifeless life.

A meaningless life and a lifeless life are smooth roads to the deep and unfathomable *Inner Void.*

Divine love, healthy self-love, spiritual love, and unconditional love, forgiveness, healing, wholeness and ultimate meaning are what we need to prevent or confront and overcome the possible deep and unfathomable *Inner Void.*

The *Larger* than *Life* deep within and all around everyone of our teens, adolescents and young adults is part of what they need if they are to know why and how to:

* *heal their too often too deeply wounded innocent Inner Child,*
* *fulfill their too often too deep and unfathomable Inner Void,*
* *alleviate their too often unbearable pain of Inner Emptiness.*

Teens, adolescents and young adults' 3 steps to the *Larger* than *Life* within and all around everyone of them are:

* *true and unconditional love for all, including for their worst enemies,*

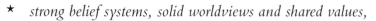

* strong belief systems, solid worldviews and shared values,
* ultimate meaning or super-meaning or meaning as divine design.

On Their Own Words: In a poem entitled
Love, Apostle Saint Paul wrote:
"If I speak in the tongue of mortals and angels,
But do not have love,
I am a noisy gong or a clanging cymbal.
If I have prophetic powers and understand
all mysteries and all knowledge,
...If I have all faith, so as to move mountains,
but don't have love, I am nothing...
Love is patient, love is kind,
love bears all things, believes all things,
hopes all things, endures all things,
Love never ends".

Once our children are open and receptive to true and unconditional love, they are more likely to have the wisdom they need to be willing and able to:

* love all those who love them,
* love all those who hate them,
* forgive all those who hurt them.

Once they are open and receptive to their loved ones and important others' strong belief systems, they will be willing and able to:

* be in touch with the Larger than Life deep in everyone of them,

- ★ be deeply touched by the *Larger* than *Life* all around everyone of them.
- ★ enjoy and share the best there is within and all around everyone of them.

Our teens, adolescents and young adults need Ultimate Meaning or Super-Meaning or Meaning as Divine Design if they are to know why and how to enjoy and share and celebrate true and long lasting Fulfillment.

7 Vital Steps to True and Long Lasting *Fulfillment*

Dear parents and community leaders, our open-minded teens, adolescents and young adults are meant to know why and how to prevent or confront and overcome the possible deep and unfathomable *Inner Void* by and through:

- ★ divine love, divine grace, divine guidance,
- ★ healthy self-love,
- ★ spiritual love,
- ★ unconditional love,
- ★ the Larger than Life within and all around everyone of them,
- ★ forgiveness, healing, wholeness, ultimate meaning, inner peace...
- ★ the emergence of their own true Self, transcendent Self, infinite Self.

CHAPTER 3

Share Long Lasting Inner Peace

The most thought provoking thing in our most thought provoking time is that we are still not thinking...
Making itself intelligible is suicide for philosophy.
(Martin Heiddeger, philosopher)

Dear Teens...Share True and Long Lasting Inner Peace

The third rock solid founding block of
All For Excellence In Education

Or the third *Vital Step* to every normal *Child's Inner Splendor*

Is true and long lasting *Inner Peace.*

True and long lasting *Inner Peace is the*
Panacea or the universal remedy

Against all man-made tragedies.

True and long lasting *Inner Peace* is the
true and long lasting *Solution* to:

* juvenile delinquency, chemical dependency...
* early and risky sexual behavior, unvanted pregnancies, child abuse...
* youth violence, domestic violence, all man-made tragedies...

A peaceful life in a peaceful world for every thinking soul,
With strong belief systems for all to hold on to,
With enough clean water for all to quench their thirst,
With enough healthy food for all to eat to live,
With a why for all to live by and a how for all to get through
Is almost all it takes us all as a whole to fight for *Peace* for all

From the inside out and from the outside in.
True and long lasting *Inner Peace* for all is vital
To true and long lasting *Peace* with one another
In every family, every street, every school, every workplace
In every community, every county, every
country, every continent...

An honest man is always a child.
(Socrates, philosopher)

Dear parents and community leaders, the third rock solid founding block of All For Excellence In Education or the third Vital Step to every normal Child's Inner Splendor is true and long lasting Inner Peace so vital to true and long lasting Peace with one another.

Dear parents and community leaders, true and long lasting *Inner Peace* for all is the *Panacea* or the universal remedy against all man-made tragedies.

As human beings, we each and all are feeble and faillible and vulnerable. To survive and thrive as social human beings, we each and all need true and long lasting:

* ⋆ *Inner Peace,*
* ⋆ *Peace with one another,*
* ⋆ *Peace within and across all cultures.*

True and long lasting *Inner Peace* so vital to true and long lasting *Peace* with one another, is:

* ⋆ *a social and a historical necessity,*
* ⋆ *a psychological necessity,*
* ⋆ *a spiritual necessity.*

True and long lasting *Inner Peace* for all is one of the true and long lasting *Solutions* to modern man's biggest problem.

Depth psychologist, Carl G. Jung, tells us that modern man's biggest problem is not a personality problem. Modern man's biggest problem is a religious and/or spiritual problem.

Our strong belief systems or spiritually ways of being are some of our first and best ways to *Ultimate Meaning or Super-Meaning or Meaning as Divine Design*.

The Problem

The absence of true and long lasting *Inner Peace* is at the root cause of the ineffable and unbearable possible *Pain* of *Inner Emptiness*. And no one and nothing material can help us alleviate the ineffable and unbearable possible *Pain of Inner Emptiness*.

The ineffable and unbearable possible *Pain* of *Inner Emptiness* exposes certain teens, adolescents and young adults to what world famous neurologist, psychiatrist and logo-therapist, Viktor Emil Frankl, calls:

*   ★ *the existential vacuum,*
*   ★ *the existential frustration,*
*   ★ *the frustrated will to meaning, to power, to money, to pleasure.*

Our teens, adolescents and young adults' exposures to *the existential vacuum, to the existential frustration and to the frustrated will to meaning, power, money and pleasure* are at the root causes of their:

★ *juvenile delinquency, chemical dependency...*
★ *early and risky sexual behavior, unwanted pregnancies...*
★ *depression, aggression, youth violence...*

The Solution

True and long lasting *Inner Peace* is younth's smoothest road to:

★ *their in-depth self-discovery, one of their lifelong greatest discoveries,*
★ *their will and skills and wisdom to be true to their own true identity,*
★ *their will and skills and wisdom to become who truly they are meant to be.*

True and long lasting *Inner Peace* for all is our teens, adolescents and young adults' pathway to *Oneness* with full *Self-awareness:*

★ *oneness with their loved ones and important others...*
★ *oneness between their knowledge/skills and innate talent,*
★ *oneness between what they have to do and what they are called to do,*
★ *oneness with their own true Self, transcendent Self, infinite Self.*

Teens, adolescents and young adults' openness to *Oneness* with all, including their worst enemies, is another true measure of their *Excellence In Education.*

How powerful it is to be wise enough to love unconditionally all, including our hurtful loved ones and important others.

With true and long lasting *Inner Peace* with their own true *Self,* open-minded teens, adolescents and young adults are likely to be well equipped and ready to enjoy and share *Peace* with almost everyone else including their hurtful friends and foes.

People who are truly in *Peace* with their own true *Self* do know why and how to be in *Peace* with almost everyone else.

Their Own Story: *Once upon a time, there was a Zen Master named Hakuin. Hakuin had many disciples who came to him for spiritual awakening and guidance.*

But one day, a girl next door gets pregnant. When confronted by her angry parents, she accused Hakuin, the Zen Master. The parents of the girl came to Hakuim and told him: "You are the father of our daughter's unborn child."

"Is that so?" was all Hakuin asked.

Then, the Zen Master lost his name and fame and reputation. His disciples abandoned him. Yet, Hakuin remained unmoved. He continues to live as if nothing has ever happened to him.

After the birth of the baby, the angry grandparents brought him to Hakuin and said, "You are the father, you take care of him."

Hakuin took good care of the baby. But a year later, the teenage mother confessed to her parents that the real father was not Hakuin but a young man working at the butcher's shop.

The grandparents came back to Hakuin in great distress, they apologized and asked for forgiveness. "We are really sorry. We came to take the baby back. Our daughter confessed that you are not the father."

"Is that so?" was all Hakuin asked, as he, the Zen Master, handed the baby back to his grandparents. (readapted from Eckhart Tolle's book "A New Earth: Awakening To Your Life Purpose.")

To *Educate All For Excellence* is to inspire all children to know why and how to:

* ★ *rely on their own self-mastery,*
* ★ *learn from their own self-mastery,*
* ★ *build upon their own self-mastery.*

Open-minded teens, adolescents and young adults can learn about the powerful life giving and life animating power of self-mastery by and through *fairy-tales, proverbs, maxims and imagined and true stories of all people with true and long lasting powers.*

At a certain level, the deepest level,
At a certain level, the highest level,
The whole world seems to be the same world,
All men and all women of the whole world
Seem to be the same important men and women
Of the same important family: *the Human Family.*

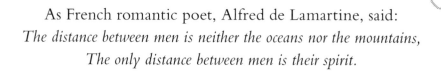

As French romantic poet, Alfred de Lamartine, said:
The distance between men is neither the oceans nor the mountains,
The only distance between men is their spirit.

The Problem

There are many major barriers to true and long lasting *Inner Peace*. Among them are what neurologist and logo-therapist, Viktor E. Frankl, calls:

* ★ *the frustrated will to meaning,*
* ★ *the frustrated will to power,*
* ★ *the frustrated will to money,*
* ★ *the frustrated will to pleasure at its lowest level.*

These 4 major barriers to true and long lasting *Inner Peace* are at the root causes of some of the world's most wide spread unbearable *Pain* of *Inner Emptiness.*

When teens, adolescents and young adults face the unbearable possible *Pain* of their *Inner Emptiness,* no one and nothing material can help them confront and overcome it:

* ★ *no deep knowledge, no vast practical skills, no dream jobs...*
* ★ *no promising future, no titles, no material possessions...*
* ★ *no name, no fame, no popularity, no cheerful fans...*

The Solution

We must help our open-minded teens, adolescents and young adults to know why and how to prevent or confront and overcome the unbearable possible *Pain* of *Inner Emptiness* by and through their openness and receptivity to:

* *divine love, divine grace, divine guidance...*
* *ultimate meaning or super-meaning or meaning as divine design,*
* *healthy self-love, spiritual love, unconditional love, forgiveness, healing...*

Those who face the unbearable *Pain* of *Inner Emptiness* may create what world famous depth psychologist and psychoanalyst, Carl G. Jung, calls the *Empty Center.*

In the *Empty Center,* there is:

* *no theology, no ideology, no philosophy of life...*
* *no time tested ways of life, no shared values, no solid worldviews...*
* *no honesty, no integrity, no humility, no compassion, no sympathy...*

In the Empty Center, all there is, is:

* *I, me, myself, mine...*
* *my way or no way,*
* *megalomania, self aggrandizement.*

The major preoccupation of people victims of the *Empty Center* is:

* *does it work?*
* *what is in it for me?*
* *how can I get the best and the most out of it?*

The Empty Center is a too limiting and misleading way of life. The *Empty Center* is at the root cause of so many psychological, social, cultural, political, economic, marital...problems around the world.

Their Own Story: *Hilter's personal life has no warm, no charm, no weight...Hitler has no education, no preoccupation, no dignity, no love, no faith, no spouse, no kids...*

Apart from his political ambition, Hitler's personal life has been an empty and an unhappy one. Inner emptiness and unhappiness happen to anyone including those with high power position and material possessions.

Hitler did not know how to give and receive love. He had been with few women. He treated them badly. They felt unloved and unhappy. For instance, Gely Raubel did committe suicide. Eva Browm attempted twice to committe suicide. "He only needs you for certains purposes," sadly said Eva Brown.

Hitler was an extremely shy guy. When he rose to power, he killed Rohm, the only intimate friend he ever had. He enjoyed sitting for hours with his subordinate staff...

But he alone did the talking. He avoids real friendship. His relationship with men like Goring, Goebbels and Himmler remained cool, remote, business like and almost meaningless. (re-adapted from Edward Osers's "The Meaning of Hitler, His Use of Power: His success and Failures")

The Problem

We live, at the same time, in a material world and in a spiritual world. When we try, as we so often do, to live as if our whole world were merely material:

* ★ *we wound the already too vulnerable innocent Inner Child in us,*
* ★ *we deepen the already too deep and unfathomable Inner Void,*
* ★ *we worsen the already unbearable Pain of Inner Emptiness.*

This is why and how so many people around so many corners of the world are caught up and held hostages by the world wide spread:

* ★ *frustrated will to meaning,*
* ★ *frustrated will to power,*
* ★ *frustrated will to money,*
* ★ *frustrated will to pleasure at its lowest level.*

A meaningful life, a powerful life, an abundant life and a joyful life are all vital to our ability to survive and thrive as human beings. They all are crucial to the quality of our day-to-day life well-being.

But they do have little or nothing to do with our spiritual needs and our inner well-being.

The Solution

As spiritual beings, our teens, adolescents and young adults have deep needs and ultimate longings no one and nothing material can help them satisfy.

A truly meaningful life, powerful life, abundant life and a joyful life require more than what the material world can offer. In addition to their material needs from their material world, our children have other deep needs and ultimate longings to be satisfied by and through only true and long lasting:

* *fulfillment,*
* *inner peace,*
* *ultimate meaning or meaning as divine design.*

To live a meaningful life and a peaceful life in a meaningful and a peaceful world, we need to know why and how to enjoy and share a day-to-day living conducive to ultimate meaning or super-meaning or meaning as a divine design.

For instance, children' unsatisfied educational need for *Belonging* can be an open door to their:

* *fear of life,*
* *blind conformity,*

* *mediocrity, co-dependence...*

Children' unsatisfied need for relative *Independence* can be another open door to their:

* *fear of death,*
* *way as the only way,*
* *aggressiveness, guilty feelings.*

As already said, the 3 deadliest educational diseases are what psychologist of Artistic Creativity, Otto Rank, and what psychoanalyst, Carl G. Jung, call:

* *the fear of life, (Otto Rank)*
* *the fear of death, (Otto Rank)*
* *the empty center. (Carl G. Jung)*

People may gain the whole world with
a loss of their own soul,
They may have it all and still feel totally Empty on the Inside,
They may feel lost in the deep and dark abyss of nothingness.
Therein, they may live a meaningless and a lifeless life,
Therein, they may live as mere walking copses,
Despite all their power position and material possessions.

Their Own Story: Hilter's way was the only way. On November 23, 1939, Hitler confessed it when said that:

"...I must, in all modesty, list my own person irreplaceable. Neither a military nor a civilian could take my place...the fate of the Reich depends on me alone, I shall act accordingly."

Hitler's true and single ambition was to subordinate Germany and the rest of the world to his unstable personality and megalomania. He was characterized by his faithlessness, ruthlessness, cruelty and vindictiveness and lack of self-criticism.

Hitler's inner void was deep and unfathomable. His inner emptiness was ineffable and unbearable. He was always full of his own false self-imposed self-defeating self.

After the failed attempt on his life, Hitler confessed his Inner Emptiness when he said:

"If my life comes to an end, then for me personally...I can say this...it would have been merely liberation from worries, sleeplessness and grave nervous diseases." (re-adapted from Edward Osers' "Hitler Use of Power: His Success and Failures."

The spiritual world requires each and everyone of us to fight with all our might for:

- ⋆ *a meaningful life,*
- ⋆ *a peaceful life,*
- ⋆ *a purposeful life.*

The Problem

The feeling of the ineffable and unbearable possible *Pain of Inner Emptiness* makes life miserable for anyone, including for:

* ★ *the knowledgeable,*
* ★ *the powerful,*
* ★ *the rich and the famous...*

It is impossible for teens, adolescents and young adults to enjoy and share a meaningful life in a meaningless world when they live a meaningless and a lifeless life.

The Solution

True and long lasting *Inner Peace* is the true and long lasting solution to the ineffable and unbearable possible Pain of *Inner Emptiness*. If we are to prevent or confront and overcome successfully the unbearable possible *Pain of Inner Emptiness*, we need to know why and how to be in true and long lasting *Peace* with:

* ★ *our own true Self,*
* ★ *our loved ones and important others' true Self,*
* ★ *everyone else's true Self.*

People, all over the world, are doing the best they know how to enjoy and share:

* *a meaningful life,*
* *a peaceful life,*
* *a powerful life,*
* *an abundant life.*

To succeed, they need to know why and how to enjoy and share a meaningful life beyond meaning as simple:

* *social construct,*
* *personal construct,*
* *dialogical encounter between social and personal construct.*

7 Vital Steps to True and Long lasting Inner Peace

Dear parents and community leaders, if our teens, adolescents and young adults are to enjoy and share true and long lasting *Inner Peace* so vital to Peace with one another, we must inspire them to know why and how to:

* *love truly, live fully alive...*
* *forgive, forget, heal, be whole...*
* *identify their own true identity,*
* *be true to their own true identity,*
* *become who truly they are meant to be,*
* *enjoy and share a meaningful life, a peaceful life, a purposeful life...*
* *re-align what they have to do to what they are called to do.*

PART II

All For Excellence In Education
3 Building Blocks

Dear parents and community leaders,
All For Excellence In Education (AFEIE)
3 rock solid building blocks
Or the second 3 *Vital Steps* to every
normal *Child's Inner Splendor* are:

★ the *Unity* between children' life unavoidable *Conflicts,*
★ the *Balance* between children' *External Authority and Inner Autonomy,*
★ the *Harmony* between children' natural pairs of personal *Inner Opposites.*

Dear parents and community leaders,
There is a natural and normal ongoing *Conflict*
Between teens, adolescents and young adults deep need':

★ *for Belonging* and for relative *Independence,*
★ for personal *Inclination* and their loved ones' *Expectations,*
★ *for their Persona-mask* and their true and total *Personality.*

CHAPTER 4

Unify Life's Unavoidable Conflicts

From the living comes death, and from the dead, life...
the stream of creation and decay never stands still...
Construction and destruction and destruction and
construction...this is the norm which rules in every
circle of natural life from the smallest to the greatest.
(Heraclitus, pre-Socratic philosopher)

Dear Teens...See your Adversity as a Great University

The first rock solid building block of
All For Excellence In Education
Or the fourth *Vital Step* to every normal *Child's Inner Splendor*
Is the *Unity* between your lifelong unavoidable *Conflicts*.
One of your best life learning experiences
is to know why and how
To face constructively your life
unavoidable greatest adversities.
When you know why and how to face
your life's greatest adversities,
You may reach the most powerful life
giving and life animating power,
You may activate the most sensitive
strings of your innermost being,
Therein lie, often dormant, your *Cosmic and/or Larger than Life*
Insight, inspiration, vision...so vital to
the actualization of your:

* new and better ways of seeing the world,
* new and better ways of being in the world,
* new and better ways of contributing to the world.

When you face constructively your life greatest adversities,
You will be willing and able and ready
to know why and how to:

* *awaken the positive side of the sleeping giant* in you that is in
no other,
* *treasure the priceless inner treasure in you* that is in no other,

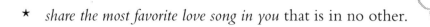

★ *share the most favorite love song in you* that is in no other.

Build a two-way learning road between
your two learning worlds,
Some of the world greatest wisdom gurus tell us that:

★ *the common ground is our ideal playground,*
★ *the win-win game of life is our life's ideal winning game,*
★ *the middle is our ideal pathway to wisdom.*

No one can ever step twice in the same river
for the water is not the same water
and he is not the same person.
(Heraclitus, a pre-Socratic philosopher)

Dear parents and community leaders, the first rock solid building block of All For Excellence In Education or the fourth Vital Step to every normal Child's Inner Splendor is the Unity between the natural and normal life unavoidable Conflicts.

Dear parents and community leaders, there is a natural and normal ongoing *Conflict* between children':

- ★ educational need for *Belonging* and for relative *Independence,*
- ★ personal *Inclination* and their loved ones' *Expectations,*
- ★ *Persona-mask* and their true and total *Personality.*

How parents help children handle their life natural and normal and unavoidable *Conflicts* determines their:

- ★ *emotional balance, mental stability, healthy growth...*
- ★ *openness to honesty, integrity, humility, sociability...*
- ★ *receptivity to compassion, passion, trust, intimacy...*

Open-minded teens, adolescents and young adults need to know why and how to *Unify* their natural and normal life's unavoidable ongoing *Conflicts.*

Psychoanalysts tell us that the tension between life unavoidable *Conflicts* is the source of the psychic energies. The greater the tension, the more abundant the psychic energies.

The Problem

In the animal kingdom, the strongest and the fittest are the more likely to survive. In the human kingdom, the *Unity* between our life's natural and normal unavoidable *Conflicts* hold the too often untold *Secret* of the mutual mutation of the *Opposites* into something:

* ★ *more,*
* ★ *bigger,*
* ★ *better.*

For instance, the *Harmony* between our *Consciousness* and our *Unconscious* is at the source of the emergence of our true, transcendent, infinite *Self.*

Our true *Self* involves but encompasses, by far:

* ★ *our social induced self,*
* ★ *our personal induced self,*
* ★ *our dialogical encounter induced self.*

The *Unity* between children' first and second deepest educational needs for *Belonging* and for relative *Independence* is the first rock solid building block of their entire educational journey.

The first and one of the worst root causes of all educational failures at all levels is the *Disharmony* between children' two first deepest and equally important educational needs for *Belonging* and for relative *Independence*.

The *Imbalance* between children' two first deepest educational needs for *Belonging* and for relative *Independence* may compromise and undermine their entire educational journey.

The Solution

Children' two first deepest educational needs for *Belonging* and for relative *Independence* are two equally important educational needs.

These two first deepest educational needs for Belonging and for relative Independence must be:

* ★ *regarded as two equally important educational needs,*
* ★ *treated as two equally important educational needs,*
* ★ *rewarded as two equally important educational needs.*

The Balance between children' first deepest educational need for Belonging and their second deepest educational need for relative Independence is one of their lifelong most vital but too often missing Life Saving Signals on their long road to All For Excellence In Education.

The 3 major barriers to the *Unity* between children' two first deepest educational needs are due parents and other educators' negligence to:

- ★ *see them as two equally important educational needs,*
- ★ *treat them as two equally important educational needs,*
- ★ *reward them as two equally important educational needs.*

Indeed, the existence and true nature and deep needs of the innocent *Inner Child* in every child are not as obvious as those of the *Outer Child*.

Besides, children' two first deepest educational needs do not start exactly at the same time during their growing up process.

Their first deepest educational need for *Belonging* starts early on in their life. Their need for *Belonging* can be felt probably even before their birth. As the old saying goes, *a child is educated 20 years before birth.*

While children' second deepest educational need for relative *Independence* starts slowly and gradually along with their growing up process.

Children' need for *Belonging* is also the most seriously taking care of as:

- ★ *a social and cultural necessity,*
- ★ *a psychological necessity,*
- ★ *a socio-professional necessity.*

For instance, children' need for *Belonging* is taken care of by:

* *the whole family,*
* *the whole community,*
* *the whole country.*

While children' need for relative *Independence* is often left to the sole initiative of:

* *immature children,*
* *inexperienced children,*
* *children on their own rocky road to education as an awakening process.*

Only emotionally balanced and mentally stable teens, adolescents and young adults may know why and how to navigate smoothly between:

* *their first deepest educational need for Belonging,*
* *and their second deepest educational need for relative Independence.*

Parents with their own healthy innocent *Inner Child*, inspiring teachers, emotionally stable friends, true lovers, spiritual gurus and motivational speakers may also inspire certain children to know why and how to:

* *identify their own true identity,*
* *be true to their own true identity,*
* *become who truly they are meant to be.*

Children with good behavior and perfect school attendance and straight A's in school are often praised and well rewarded in many different ways by all educators at all levels.

But teens, adolescents and young adults with some originality and natural gift and high creativity may often be:

* *left alone on their own,*
* *or even scorn off as outsiders,*
* *or ignored and silenced.*

The first group may run the risk of:

* *the fear of life,*
* *blind conformity,*
* *mediocrity, co-dependence.*

The second group may run the risk of:

* *the fear of death,*
* *self-fishness,*
* *aggressiveness, guilty feelings...*

As parents and educators, we must inspire all open-minded teens, adolescents and young adults to know why and how to navigate smoothly and successfully between their first and second deepest equally important educational needs:

* *for Belonging,*
* *and for relative Independence.*

Inspiring people are what Chicago based preacher, Robb Thomson, calls "tomorrow's people." Contrary to what he calls "yesterday's peole" and "today's people;" "tomorrow's people" are the ones who see in a child more than the eye can see.

They are also the ones who inspire the child to see in himself what they saw. For instance, they may help the child to know why and how to:

* *awaken the positive side of his/her sleeping giant that is in no other,*
* *treasure his/her own priceless inner treasure that is in no other,*
* *share his/her most favorite love song that has never been sung before.*

> *Blessed is he who has found his own job,*
> *ask him for no other blessedness.*
> *(Thomas Carlyle)*

The Problem

Teens, adolescents and young adults have to go through a constant struggle between their need for *Belonging* and their need for relative *Independence*.

Too often, they may choose to enjoy their need for *Belonging* at the detriment of their need for relative *Independence*. In doing so, they may undermine their entire educational journey. They may even compromise:

* their *mental stability,*
* *their emotional balance,*
* *their healthy growth.*

The Solution

To solve the natural and normal ongoing *Conflict* between children's first deepest educational need for *Belonging* and their second deepest educational need for relative *Independence* is to inspire them to know why and how to:

* *satisfy, ideally at same time, their two first deepest educational needs,*
* *navigate smoothly between their two first deepest educational needs,*
* *enjoy at the same time their two first deepest educational needs.*

For instance, open-minded teens, adolescents and young adults need to know why and how to build a two-way learning road between:

* *their Outer Child and their Inner Child,*
* *their External learning world and their Internal learning world,*
* *their Knowledge reproduction and their new Knowledge production.*

To succeed, they need to know why and how to:

* *identify their own true identity,*

★   *strive for the knowledge/skills relevant to their innate talent,*
    ★   *become who truly they are meant to be.*

They also need to know why and how to build a two-way learning road between:

    ★   *the two learners in every student,*
    ★   *the two learning worlds in every teaching-learning environment,*
    ★   *the two learning outcomes in every teaching-learning process.*

The Problem

The unresolved *Conflict* between the two first deepest educational needs for *Belonging* and for relative *Independence* is the first and one of the worst root causes of:

    ★   *the parenting 3 massive mistakes,*
    ★   *the dark and ugly side of the Personal Unconscious,*
    ★   *the huge gap between the Persona-mask and the true Personality,*
    ★   *all educational failures at all levels and all man-made tragedies.*

The Solution

The two-way teaching-learning road between children' need for *Belonging* and for relative *Independence* is one of the solutions of:

    ★   *the parenting 3 massive mistakes,*
    ★   *the 3 deadliest educational diseases,*
    ★   *all educational failures at all levels.*

Children' need for *Belonging* must be satisfied by and through their loved ones and important others':

* *time tested ways of life,*
* *shared values,*
* *solid worldviews.*

Children' need for relative *Independence* must be satisfied by and through their:

* *in-depth self-discovery,*
* *will and skills and wisdom to be true to their own true identity,*
* *will and skills and wisdom to become who truly they are meant to be.*

The Problem

To try to satisfy children' need for *Belonging* at the detriment of their need for relative *Independence* may expose certain of them to:

* *the fear of life,*
* *blind conformity,*
* *mediocrity, co-dependence...*

To allow teens, adolescents and young adults to be focused on their need for relative *Independence* at the detriment of their need for *Belonging* may expose them to:

* *be the victims of the fear of death,*
* *see their own way as the only way,*
* *be aggressive, violent with guilty feelings.*

The Solution

To Balance children' need for *Belonging* and for relative *Independence* is one of the first *Vital* but too often missing *Life Saving Signal* on their long road to Excellence In Education.

Young children need to know why and how to enjoy and share their educational need for *Belonging* by adopting and avoiding what their loved ones and important others consider:

* *what is right and what is wrong,*
* *what is good and what is bad,*
* *what is desirable and what is undesirable.*

Young children need to know why and how to enjoy and share their need for relative *Independence* by and through:

* *their in-depth self-discovery...*
* *their true identity, uniqueness, natural gift...*
* *their effort to become who truly they are meant to be...*

To succeed, they need to know why and how to satisfy, ideally at the same time, their need for *Belonging* and for relative *Independence*. Otherwise, they may run the risk of facing one of the 3 following deadliest educational diseases or what psychologist, Otto Rank, and depth psychologist, Carl G. Jung, call:

* *the Fear of Life, (Otto Rank)*
* *the Fear of Death, (Otto Rank)*
* *the Empty Center, (Carl G. Jung)*

CHAPTER 5

Balance Authority and Inner Autonomy

What lies behind us and what lies in front of us
are small matters compared to what lies within us...
A man should learn and watch that gleam of light
that flashes across his mind from within
more than the luster of the firmament.
(Ralph Waldo Emerson, theologian and essayist)

Dear Teens...Love Truly to Live Fully Alive,

The second rock solid building block of
All For Excellence In Education
Or the fifth *Vital Step* to every normal *Child's Inner Splendor*
Is the *Balance* between their loved ones and important others'
Expectations and their own personal *Inclination.*
Love all your loved ones and important others with true love,
Love your own self with healthy self-love,
Build a two-way learning road between
your two learning worlds.
Love all those who love you,
Love all those who hate you,
Forgive all those who hurt you,
Remember, only hurting people hurt other people.
Learn, at the same time, from your two learning worlds,
Your two learning worlds are two equally
important learning worlds.
Dear teens, adolescents and young adults,
You are, at the same time, made and self made,
You are what your *Creator and* your
loved ones want you to be,
You are also what you make your own self to be.
Your need for *Belonging* is your first deepest educational need,
Your need for *Independence* is your second
deepest educational need,
The *Balance* between your two first deepest educational needs
Determines great deal of the quality of
your entire educational journey,
The steadier their *Balance,* the stronger your mental stability...

The middle is the pathway to wisdom.
(Jalal U. Rumi, mystic poet)

Dear parents and community leaders, the second rock solid building block of All For Excellence In Education or the fifth Vital Step to every normal Child's Inner Splendor is the Balance between children' personal Inclination and their loved ones and important others' Expectations, Demands and Requirements.

When it comes to *All For Excellence In Education:*

* ★ *hard work alone won't work,*
* ★ *pure logic alone won't help,*
* ★ *analytical intelligence alone won't crack down the Excellence code.*

On Their Own Words: Depth psychologist and psychoanalyst, Carl G. Jung, tell us that:

No one can know what the ultimate things are. We must therefore take them as we experience them. And if such experience helps to make life healthier, more beautiful and more satisfactory to yourself and to those you love, you may safely say: "This was the grace of God."

It is said that the whole science of the whole world won't help us be a good artist if we do not have the artistic gut.

For instance:

* In writing, there have been many world great writers, but there are few like Shakespeare, Dante, Goethe, Victor Hugo...
* In music, there have been many world great musicians, but there are few like Mozart, Beethoven...
* In soccer, there have been many world great players, but there are few like Pele...
* In basketball, there have been many world great players, but there are few like Micheal Jordan...
* In baseball, there have been many world great players, but there are few like Roberto Clemente...

All For Excellence In Education is a two-way bridge building process, bridge between learners':

* *reason and emotion,*
* *logic and intuition,*
* *hard work and smart work.*

Open-minded teens, adolescents and young adults need to know why and how to navigate smoothly and successfully between:

* their loved ones' *Expectations* and their own personal *Inclination,*
* their loved ones' *Authority* and their own *inner Autonomy,*
* their loved ones' *Requirements* and their own dominant talent.

The Problem

Children face a natural and normal ongoing *Conflict* between:

* ⭐ *their Outer Child and their Inner Child,*
* ⭐ *their External learning world and their Internal learning world,*
* ⭐ *their Knowledge reproduction and their new Knowledge production.*

Some of the world's great pioneers of education, such as John Locke, tell us that the child's mind is like a *blank slate or a tabula rasa.* In the beginning, there is nothing in it to begin with.

Such a worldview on education implies that children are educated by and through their loved ones and important others':

* ⭐ *time tested ways of life,*
* ⭐ *shared values,*
* ⭐ *solid worldviews.*

Yes, Education is first a Socializing process.

To satisfy children' need for *Belonging* is to inspire them know why and how to enjoy and share their loved ones and important others':

* ⭐ *time tested ways of life,*
* ⭐ *shared values,*
* ⭐ *solid worldviews.*

But other still world great pioneers of education, such as Socrates, Plato, Confucius, Jean Jack Rousseau...tell us that every normal child has all the potentialities to become all he/she is meant to be.

For true believers, every child is divinely/spiritually meant to be:

* *all loving,*
* *all knowing,*
* *all powerful.*

Such a second worldview on education implies that all open-minded teens, adolescents and young adults are meant to know why and how to:

* *awaken the positive side of their own inner splendor that is in no other,*
* *treasure their own priceless inner treasure that is in no other,*
* *sing their own life's most favorite love song that is in no other.*

Yes, Education is also an Awakening process.

It is said that when profession coincides with vocation, the rest is illumination.

Children' knowledge is acquired. Children' skills are acquired. They have to struggle hard, day and night, to get their required knowledge and skills.

But children' talent is a divine given gift. Children' talent is a natural gift. Their talent cannot be taught. Their talent cannot be bought. Their talent is to be caught. To catch their innate talent, they need to know why and how to:

* *learn, at the same time, from their External and Internal learning worlds,*
* *strive for the very knowledge/skills relevant to their innate talent,*
* *match what they have to do to what they are truly called to do.*

Once they succeed, they may have the will and skills and wisdom they need to know why and how to:

* *awaken their own Inner Splendor,*
* *treasure their own priceless Inner Treasure that is in no other,*
* *share their life's most favorite Love Song that has never been sung before.*

Children' *Innate Talent* lies, often dormant, deep down within each and everyone of them. Let inspire them to know why and how to awaken the positive side of the sleeping giant deep within each and everyone of them.

The problem

There is always an ongoing *Conflict* between:

* *Education as a Socializing process,*
* *and Education as an Awakening process.*

To give more importance to one at the detriment of the other may compromise the quality of children' entire educational journey.

Have you ever seen and known or heard about some very polite and conformist grown up children who still live in the basement of their parents' house?

Have you ever seen and known or heard about some of the world famous stars who live a loveless and lonely and miserable life because their way has always to be the only way?

Dear parents and community leaders, my own way as the only way may be the loneliest and most miserable way in life, in education, in marriage...

The day-to-day social life is best lived in the middle, the ideal pathway to wisdom.

The focus of Education as a *Socializing* process is knowledge and skills reproduction.

The focus of Education as an *Awakening* process is new knowledge and skills production.

There is no new knowledge and skills production without knowledge and skills reproduction.

But there is more to new knowledge and skills production than simple knowledge skills reproduction.

The Solution

To enjoy and share, at the same time, Education as a *Socializing* process and Education as an *Awakening* process is to build a two-way teaching-learning road between:

* *the two learners in every student,*
* *the two teaching-learning worlds,*
* *the two teaching-learning outcomes in every teaching-learning process.*

All children in general and all open-mended teens, adolescents and young adults in particular need to know why and how to enjoy and share their loved ones and important others':

* *time tested ways of life,*
* *shared values,*
* *solid worldviews.*

No child is meant to start everything from scratch. No child is expected to start everything from scratch.

As social human beings, all children are, in some degree, meant to be what their loved ones and important others want them to be...

Education is first a Socializing process.

But for all true believers, every normal child has also all the potentialities to become all he/she is divinely/spiritually meant to be.

For such second educational worldview, education involves but encompasses the:

* ★ *the simple knowledge and skills reproduction,*
* ★ *the simple Socializing process.*

The *Awakening* process is Education's second vital function.

Education as an *Awakening* process is based on the strong belief system that every normal child has all the potentialities to:

* ★ *awaken the positive side of their sleeping giant within that is in no other,*
* ★ *treasure their own priceless inner treasure that is in no other,*
* ★ *share their life's most favorable love song that has never been sung before.*

Their own Story: In the streets of Athen, ancient Greek philosopher, Socrates used to ask questions to all people of all walks of life. He did not ask them questions to see what and how much they knew. He asked them questions to inspire them to be fully aware and deeply convinced that they each and all have their own sleeping giant deep within that needs to be awakened, enjoyed, shared and celebrated.

Balance External Authority and Inner Autonomy

All teens, adolescents and young adults need to know why and how to behave at the same time as:

* ★ *social human beings,*
* ★ *individual human beings.*
* ★ *spiritual beings.*

They each and all need to know why and how to act and interact and react at the same time as:

* ★ *social human beings,*
* ★ *individual human beings,*
* ★ *spiritual beings.*

Depth psychologists tell us that the psychological meaning of our *Collective Unconscious* is that our psyche has a personal nature. Our psyche's personal nature is called the psychology of the person. The psychology of the person causal factors are regarded as wholly in personal nature.

Therefore, we each and all need to know why and how to accept and respect and protect our own uniqueness so vital to the identification of:

* our innate talent,
* our natural calling,
* our dominant talent.

However, none of our personal psychological factors can deny the existence of an *apriori* common to all men and all women of the past and the present world.

Our *apriori* personal factors are indeed universal. They are common to all men and to all women of all time. The *apriori* has a significant impact on our personal psychology.

On the one hand, we each are, to some degree, unique.

On the other hand, we each have, to some degree, something in common with all the men and all the women of the whole world.

To some degree, we each are, at the same time, unique and universal.

For instance, our instincts are impersonal. Our instincts are universally distributed. Our instincts are common to all men and to all other animals. Our instincts are universal hereditary factors. They have a dynamic and motivating character, which often fails to reach our conscious attitude.

As social human beings, our loved ones and important others' *Expectations, Demands and Requirements* are vital components of our *Education as a Socializing* process.

Open-minded teens, adolescents and young adults need to know why and how to:

- *make a difference between what is right and what is wrong,*
- *choose what is right and avoid what is wrong,*
- *rely on and build upon the desirable and run away from the undesirable.*

The need for *External Authority* is a social and a historical necessity. Power, structure and order are as old as the oldest human families. Power, order and structure are vital to our:

- *family stability, viability and social harmony.*
- *peace with one another,*
- *peace within and across all cultures.*

CHAPTER 6

Harmonize the Personal Inner Opposites

...there is but one cause of human failure.
And that is man's lack of faith in his true self.
(William James, psychologist and philosopher)

Dear Teens...Harmonize your
Personal Inner Opposites

The third rock solid building block of
All For Excellence In Education
Or the sixth *Vital Step* to every normal *Child's Inner Splendor*
Is the *Harmony* between the natural and normal pairs
Of your personal inner *Opposites.*
You are your own best friend; you can
be your own worst enemy,
The choice is all yours; please, choose wisely.
Enjoy, share and celebrate in-depth self-discovery,
In-depth self-discovery is one of your
lifelong greatest discoveries.

Dear teens, adolescents and young adults,
Your healthy self-love is your smoothest and straightest road
To your most inspiring universal heritage,
Your healthy self-love is your best way to your higher *Self,*
Your higher *Self* is your vehicle into
the best there is in the world,
Your higher *Self* is your best way to a more meaningful life
In a more meaningful and peaceful
world for every thinking soul.
Accept, respect and protect your own
and each other's *Inner Child;*
Forget yesterday, your yesterday is gone for good,
Do not worry about tomorrow, your tomorrow is not yet,
Enjoy today, your day-to-day life's smooth flow.
Listen to the ineffable melody of the music within you,
Look for the diamond mine in your own front yard,
Refuse to die "with the music still within you."

*When the heart is cracked open, we access
the most profound human secret of life
and that is the secret of your true identity.*
(Neale Donald Walsh, spiritual guru)

*Dear parents and community leaders, the third rock solid building block
of All For Excellence In Education or the sixth Vital Step to every
normal Child's Inner Splendor is the Harmony between the natural and
normal pairs of the personal inner Opposites in everyone of us.*

Depth psychologist, Carl G. Jung, said that everyone has to go
through a struggle between the natural and normal pairs of our
own personal inner *Opposites,* that is:

* ★ our *Consciousness and Unconscious,*
* ★ our *Ego and Shadow,*
* ★ our *Persona-mask and true and total Personality.*

Psychologically, the healthy, happy and vibrant teens, adolescents
and young adults have to go through the same struggle as the
helpless, the hopeless and the homeless teens, adolescents and
young adults do.

Deep on the inside, we each and all are psychologically the
same human beings. We have to go through the same struggle
between the natural and normal pairs of our personal *Inner
Opposites.* It is the same inner struggle for:

* ★ *the well educated as well as for the non educated,*

* *the rich and the famous as well as for the poor and the anonymous,*
* *the true believers as well as for the non believers.*

The stronger the tension between the pairs of our personal inner *Opposites,* the more abundant our psychic energies. Every human being has to go through the Tensions and Contradictions between:

* *their Consciousness and their Unconscious,*
* *their Ego and their Shadow,*
* *the Persona-mask and their true and total Personality.*

The *Harmony* between teens, adolescents and young adults' natural and normal pairs of personal inner *Opposites* is vital to:

* *their mental stability,*
* *their emotional balance,*
* *their healthy growth.*

The *Harmony* between their natural and normal pairs of inner *Opposites* is what teens, adolescents and young adults need first if they are to know why and how to enjoy and share the wisdom they need to:

* *achieve in-depth self-discovery, one of their lifelong greatest discoveries,*
* *be true to their own true identity,*
* *become who truly they are meant to be.*

The Principle of Inner Opposites

The principle of inner *Opposites* is universally known. It is known throughout mankind's history. For instance, the central view of Hinduism is to achieve *"freedom from the opposites."* The Yang and Yin in Chinese philosophy is to balance the male and the female. For depth psychologists, there is, to some degree, a female in every male and a male in every female.

The principle of the inner *Opposites* is our psychic way of operating. Our psyche operates by and through contrasts, conflicts, tensions and irregular oscillations from one extreme to the other.

That is the basic process by and through which our psychic energy is created. Tensions, contradictions, oscillations then balance and harmony underline our psychic energies creation and mouvements.

On Their Own Words: According to Carl G. Jung:

The greater the tension between the pairs of opposites, the greater will be the energy that comes from them...After violent oscillations at the beginning, the contradictions balance each other and gradually a new attitude develops...

The movement of our psychic energy may have many variations from one person to the other. For some individuals, it shoots off in meaningless activities. For others individuals, it goes inward and downward into the deep layers of the collective *Unconscious*. Then, it emerges in strong and strange psychological forms.

Carl G. Jung said that our psychic movement is a constant process. It is always starting and stopping. It is always going forward and backward. It is a restless and uncertain traveller who is ever seeking and seldom finding his destination.

The Collapse of the Persona

Our *Persona* is, according to Jung, a mask or a masquerade or a facade. It is a simple social *wrapping*. It is at the *Opposite side* of our true and total *Personality*.

The collapse of the *Persona* means that our psychic energy is not flowing smoothly out toward the external world. When our *Persona* collapses, it means that our psychic energy is regressing inward and downward. This is, according to Jung, a painful personal experience.

The collapse of the Persona comes from some deceptions, failures and temporary setbacks. There are two stages of the restoration of the collapsed *Persona*.

The first Stage: We make a new compromise by rebuilding a new *Persona* at a new and lower level. For instance, if we were "aiming too high," and fail, we may form a new conscious attitude or a new *Persona* at a new and lower level.

The second Stage: We may refuse to compromise and choose the inward downward flow of our psychic energies. Our psychic energies may continue to move downward to involve increasingly the deep layers of our collective *Unconscious* contents.

During the downward flow, our psychic energies may reach universal and cosmic levels. They may reach religious and spiritual questions whose answers trigger our new and better ways of:

* ★ *seeing the world,*
* ★ *being in the world,*
* ★ *contributing to the world.*

Adversity, as the old saying goes, can be our life's greatest university.

The re-integration of our true and total *Personality* must be based on a newly found strong belief system, solid worldview, spiritually way of being or philosophy of life...

The aim of our individuation process is, according to Jung, to free us from:

* ★ the social wrappings, on the one hand,
* ★ the power of our unconscious images, on the other hand.

Harmonize the Consciousness and the Unconscious

Our *Consciousness* and the *Unconscious* are one of the natural and normal pairs of our personal inner *Opposites*. They balance each other in a constant dynamic tension. In reality, they are more than inner *Opposites*. They are rather two different degrees of depth within the same psyche.

For instance, our personal *Unconscious* is the depository of the dark and ugly side of our repressed and rejected and often forgotten side of our *Personality*. That is the part of our personal life we are not proud of. That is the part of our personal life we do not want to remember, acknowledge...

The Problem

Our personal *Unconscious* defies the control of our *Conscious* attitudes. Too often, it may pop up on its own to invade our *Conscious* attitudes.

The repressed and rejected dark and ugly side of our *personal Unconscious* do not die. It does not go away. It rather lives outside the control of our *Conscious* attitudes. It pops up as *"partial autonomous systems."*

The Solution

Our psyche is a way of thinking about the world phenomena as they appear to our inner world. It is an approach to the world, which describes how the human psychic experiences the world in terms of its own natural and normal inner *Opposites*.

The Unity, Balance and Harmony between the natural and normal pairs of our personal inner Opposites is the best way to our collective unconscious or our objective psyche.

Our collective *Unconscious* is of a universal nature. It is virtually present within everyone of us. It becomes conscious only secondarily. Our collective *Unconscious* is the depository of our universal heritage.

Our personal identification with the collective psyche is our pathway to the great truth in life. The great truth of life is waiting for each and everyone of us to be discovered by and through:

* ⋆ *divine love, divine grace, divine guidance,*
* ⋆ *healthy self-love, spiritual love, unconditional love...*
* ⋆ *forgiveness, healing, wholeness, ultimate meaning...*

Our identification with the collective *Unconscious* is our pathway to:

* ⋆ *the emergence of our true, transcendent, infinite Self,*
* ⋆ *our larger than life intuition, inspiration, imagination, vision...*
* ⋆ *our compassion, passion, ability to see adversity as a great university...*

Our identification with the collective psyche is our pathway to the great treasures that lie buried in the collective *Unconscious*.

It is vital to maintain by all means our newly won connection with that primal source of our life.

On their own Words: German's philosopher, Emmanuel Kant, said:

The treasure lying within the field of dim representations, that deep abyss of human knowledge is forever beyond our reach.

Harmonize the Ego and the Shadow

Our shadow is the contents of our personal *Unconscious*. We need deep soul searching and moral courage and effort to integrate our *Personal Unconscious into our Conscious attitudes.*

To recognize our Shadow is to recognize the dark and ugly and stubborn side of our *Personality* as present and real...To succeed, we need to know why and how to confront and overcome the repressed and rejected dark and ugly side of our *Personality.*

According to Jung, in-depth self-knowledge is a painstaking fundamental effort. It takes courage, honesty and integrity. The emergence of our true *Self* is crucial to our ability to love truly, live fully alive, forgive, forget, heal and be whole.

Our *Shadow* has an emotional nature with some inner autonomy. It is obsessive and possessive. Our emotion is not something we do. Our emotion is something that happens to us. Our *Shadow* is the part of our *Personality* where our:

* *adaptation is weak,*
* *complex of inferiority is felt,*
* *uncontrolled and scarcely controllable emotions happen.*

To some degree, our *Shadow* can be assimilated by our *Conscious* personality. But our *Shadow* has features that offer the most obstinate resistance to any moral code.

Harmonize Persona and Personality

There is a natural and normal and necessary ongoing Conflict between our:

* *Persona-mask*
* *and our true and total Personality.*

Our *Persona* is the mask we wear to meet our social *Expectations, Demands and Requirements*. To meet our social *Expectations*, we may often pretend and fake and even lie to others and to ourselves.

The Problem

The larger the gap between our *Persona-mask* and our true and total *Personality,* the deeper the wound we may inflict to anyone close to us including the very innocent *Inner Child* within each and everyone of us.

The Solution

As parents and educators, we must inspire our teens, adolescents and young adults to be aware that their true and total *Personality*, though real and present, cannot be fully known and shown in their day to day life.

Their true and total *Personality* is always in the making. It is a dynamic process always in becoming.

Their *Ego* is part of their true and total *Personality*. But their *Ego* is to their true and total *Personality* what a small part is to a larger whole.

They need to know why and how to be in touch with and deeply touched by the collective *Unconscious* or their *objective psyche* if they are to know why and how to:

* *enjoy the depository of their universal heritage,*
* *share their transcendental functions,*
* *celebrate their universal heritage.*

On Their Own Words: Carl G. Jung, the depth psychologist and psychoanalyst the most quoted in this book in general and in this chapter in particular, said:

* our collective *Unconscious* is the source of our universal supply.

* our psyche is the source of the material into our *Consciousness*.
* our *Conscious* and *Unconscious* contents seldom agree.
* our collective *Unconscious* owes their existence to the universal heritage or what:

1. French anthropologist Lucien Levy-Bruhl calls *"collective representations."*
2. comparative religions studies call *"categories of imagination."*
3. some scholars call *"primordial thoughts."*
4. Carl G. Jung calls archetypes.

Dear teens, adolescents, young adults...
Be always open and receptive to your own true *Self*,
Be always true to your own true *Self*,
Be who truly you are meant to be,
Be all loving, all knowing, all powerful,
Be peaceful culture consumers,
Become mindful culture producers,
Be your own best friends,
Refuse to be your own worst enemies,
The choice is all yours, please, choose wisely.
Try to bring out the best there is deep
within and all around you,
Try to bring out the best there is deep within and all around
All your loved ones and important others.

PART III

All For Excellence In Education
3 Life Giving Powers

Dear parents and community leaders,
All For Excellence In Education (AFEIE) 3 most powerful
Life giving and life animating powers or the last 3 Vital
But too often missing Steps
To every normal Child's Inner Splendor are:

★ *peaceful culture consumption,*
★ *self-navigation,*
★ *mindful culture production.*

As social human beings, all open-minded teens, adolescents...
Are meant to know why and how to become:

★ *the peaceful culture consumers they are born to be,*
★ *the captains of their own destiny they are meant to be,*
★ *the mindful culture producers they are meant to be.*

Dear parents and community leaders,
Our open-minded teens, adolescents and young adults
Are meant to know why and how to succeed in life

By and through their *Education* as:

- ★ *a Socializing process,*
- ★ *an Awakening process,*
- ★ *a Mindful Culture Production process.*

CHAPTER 7

Inspire Peaceful Culture Consumption

There is a golden thread that runs through
the lives and the teachings
of all the prophets, seers, sages and
saviors in the world's history,
through the lives of all men and women
of truly great and lasting
power.
(Ralph Waldo Trine, bestselling author)

Dear Teens...Be the Bridge Builders
you are Meant to be

The first most powerful life giving and life animating power
Of *All For Excellence In Education* or the seventh *Vital Step*
To every normal *Child's Inner Splendor*
is *Peaceful Culture Consumption.*
Your heart-to-heart journey is one of your
life most sought after yourneys,
Your heart-to-heart journey is one of your
life most demanding journeys,
Your heart-to-heart journey is one of your
life most rewarding journeys.
Love truly, live fully alive, build a two-
way learning road between:

* *your External* learning world and your *Internal* learning
  world,
* your loved ones' *Expectations* and your own personal
  Inclination,
* your natural and normal pairs of personal inner *Opposites.*

Your true and unconditional love for
all, including your enemies,
Is your smoothest and straightest and fastest road to:

* forgiveness, healing, wholeness, compassion, passion...
* a meaningful life, a peaceful life, a lofty purpose, a
  worthy cause...
* the best there is deep within you and all around you.

When you live a meaningless life, you live a lifeless life,
When you live a lifeless life, you die while seemingly alive.
The world great religious and spiritual traditions tell us that:

* *we each and all are created at God image,*
* *we each and all are created at God likeness,*
* *God is all loving, all knowing, all powerful.*

All loving, all knowing, all powerful is who you are meant to be...

Society is the primary reality in the study of man.
First is society, then the individual person.
(Emile Durkheim, French sociologist)

Dear parents and community leaders, the first most powerful life giving and life animating power of All For Excellence In Education or the seventh Vital but too often missing Step to every normal Child's Inner Splendor is Peaceful Culture Consumption.

Every given society has a given culture,
Every given culture
Has a given educational system,
Every given educational system is the vehicle
Of a given civilization or time tested ways of life
And shared values and solid worldviews.

Society is ideally a coherent system. In a coherent social system, the role of every individual person is, to some degree, determined by the role of all the others remaining members of the same social group.

Society is the foundation of children':

* *first deepest educational need for Belonging,*
* *day-to-day life multiple relations and interactions,*
* *deep need for social and cultural integration.*

Education, as already said, is first a Socializing process.

Children are born with their first deepest educational need for *Belonging*. To survive and thrive, they need love, caring and support from their loved ones and important others.

Without their loved ones and important others' love, caring and support, children may not know why and how to enjoy and share:

- *their mental stability,*
- *their emotional balance,*
- *their healthy growth.*

Children' first deepest educational need for *Belonging* precedes and prepares their deepest Educational needs for:

- *relative Independence,*
- *Dialogical Encounter between Belonging and Independence,*
- *Self-navigation.*

Children need to know why and how to satisfy their need for *Belonging* by and through their loved ones and important others':

- *time tested ways of life,*
- *shared values,*
- *solid worldviews.*

They need to know why and how to act, interact and react as social human beings. They need to know why and how to behave as integral and important members of:

- ★ *their own family,*
- ★ *their own religious affiliation,*
- ★ *their own school system, workplace, community, county, country...*

The Problem

There is a natural, normal and necessary ongoing *Conflict* between children' first and second deepest and equally important *Educational* needs for:

- ★ *for Belonging,*
- ★ *for relative Independence.*

Without the satisfaction of their educational need for Belonging, certain teens, adolescents and young adults may behave as if they were free to:

- ★ *say whatever they want to say,*
- ★ *do whatever they want to do,*
- ★ *be whatever they want to be.*

When they do, they compromise their first deepest educational need for *Belonging.* When they do, they may undermine the quality of their entire educational journey.

Children' need for *Belonging* must be satisfied by and through their will and skills and wisdom to know why and how to accept, respect, enjoy and share their loved ones and important others':

* *time tested ways of life,*
* *shared values,*
* *solid worldviews.*

The solution to the ongoing Conflict between children' education as a Socializing process and their education as an Awakening process is to satisfy, ideally at the same time, these two equally important educational needs.

As social human beings, all open-minded teens, adolescents and young adults must be aware and deeply convinced that they each and all are, to some degree, what their loved ones and important others want them to be.

To maintain social conformity and enjoy social harmony, open-minded teens, adolescents and young adults must know why and how to make a difference between:

* *what is socially desirable and what is not,*
* *what is socially right and what is not,*
* *what is socially good and what is not.*

Something may be acceptable to a given individual person while the same thing may be forbidden by the community as a whole.

As social human beings, all children need to know that they are meant to enjoy and share:

* *in-depth social integration,*
* *in-depth cultural identity,*
* *solid social frame of references.*

As social human beings, teens, adolescents and young adults need to be aware that their *Education* is first about:

* *who truly they are as human beings,*
* *how to enjoy and share the meaning of their social life,*
* *how to enjoy and share the meaning of their personal life.*

The Problem

In our day-to-day life, *meaning* is, at the same time:

* *a social construct,*
* *a personal construct,*
* *a dialogical encounter between social and personal construct,*
* *a divine design beyond any limited and limiting human construct.*

We are, at the same time:

* *social human beings,*
* *individual human beings,*
* *and spiritual beings.*

Meaning as a simple social construct, personal construct and dialogical encounter construct do not satisfy man's deep need and longing for:

* *ultimate meaning,*
* *or super-meaning,*
* *or meaning as divine design.*

Depth psychologist, psychiatrist and psychoanalyst, Carl Gustav Jung, said that *modern man's biggest problem is not a personality problem.*

To Jung, modern man's biggest problem is a religious/spiritual problem.

A meaningful life in a meaningful world for every thinking soul involves but encompasses what the material world has to offer.

The Solution

The *Solution* to a meaningful life in a meaningful world requires:

* *ultimate meaning,*
* *or super-meaning,*
* *or meaning as a divine design.*

Dear parents and community leaders, there is no life without a living. But there is more to life than a mere living.

Living is about our daily struggle for material things and leisure and pleasure.

Life is about our deepest needs and ultimate longings for:

- ★ *a meaningful life in a meaningful world,*
- ★ *a peaceful life in a peaceful world for every thinking soul,*
- ★ *Ultimate Meaning or Meaning as Divine Design.*

To succeed, our teens, adolescents and young adults must know why and how to enjoy, share and celebrate a living conducive to a meaningful life.

For instance, our different cultures are learned almost effortlessly. But once learned, our culture is part of what makes or breaks our teens, adolescents and young adults.

Our culture can be so powerful that Chicago University professor of psychology, Mihaley C, asks to not ask what is creativity. He rather asks to ask where creativity is. Indeed, every innovation, new invention, new product or new service happen by and through:

- ★ *a specific domain,*
- ★ *a specific field,*
- ★ *a specific or a group of specific creative mind(s).*

For instance, sport is the domain, golf is the field and Tigers Wood is a creative mind in golf. But let's suppose that Tigers Wood grew up in a small village with no electricity, no running water, no golf clubs and no professional and official authorities in golf. Tigers Wood would have probably never been one of the world biggest stars in golf.

Education as a *Socializing Process* precedes and prepares children':

* *openness and receptivity to their external learning world,*
* *need for deep social and cultural integration,*
* *need for a good and a solid character,*
* *need for a stable and an agreeable personality.*

Peaceful Culture Consumption is a social necessity,
Peaceful Culture Consumption is a historical necessity,
Peaceful Culture Consumption is a psychological necessity,
Peaceful Culture consumption is vital to true and long lasting:

* inner peace,
* peace with one another and social harmony,
* peace within and across all cultures...

The Problem

The 3 major barriers to *Education as a Socializing* process are:

* *parents and important others' way as almost the only way,*
* *teens, adolescents and young adults' way as almost the only way,*
* *parents and grown up children with no common way or no way.*

Parents'...Way as almost the Only Way

Family is the first school. Family is one of the best schools. Family is the basic substratum upon which children:

* *form a good and a solid character,*
* *develop an agreeable and a stable personality,*
* *learn why and how to be honest, trustworthy, humble, compassionate...*

Parents are the first educators. Parents are among the best educators. Loving parents are likened to a psychological vitamin indispensable to their children healthy growth.

Children' loved ones and important others' time tested ways of life, shared values and solid worldviews have always been, are still and should always be, to some degree, the way.

Indeed, we each and all are inherently social human beings in nature.

However, when it comes to our grown up children, we, as both parents and educators at all levels, must understand and respect our own children' natural and normal personal *Inclination* so vital to their ability to identify:

* *their innate talent,*
* *their dominant talent,*
* *their life purpose.*

To succeed in life, our children do not have to go through all what we have been through. To succeed in life, they need rather, as early as possible, to know why and how to:

* *identify and be true to their own true identity,*
* *identify and be more focus on their own dominant talent,*
* *re-align what they have to do to what they are truly called to do.*

When loved ones and important others' way becomes almost the only way, certain teens, adolescents and young adults may not know why and how to find their way to their own second deepest and equally important educational need for relative *Independence.*

When that happens, as it so often does, these children run the risk of:

* *mere participation mystique,*
* *the Fear of Life,*
* *bind conformity, mediocrity...*

Loved ones and important others' time tested ways of life, shared values and solid worldviews are 3 smooth roads to their children' first deepest educational needs for *Belonging.*

However, children' first deepest educational need for *Belonging* is just a step, their first step on a rather long and often rocky and slippery road to their *Excellence In Education.*

Children' deep educational need for relative *Independence* is their second deepest and equally important educational need.

Their failure to know why and how to enjoy and share their second deepest educational need for relative *Independence* may expose them to:

- ★ *the fear of death,*
- ★ *aggressiveness,*
- ★ *violence and guilty feelings.*

The Solution

The win-win parenting style is a fundamental but too often missing *Life Saving Signal* on the long road to *All For Excellence In Education.*

The Middle or the ideal pathway to wisdom is the Solution to the Parenting 3 Massives Mistakes or:

- ★ *parents and important others' way as almost the only way,*
- ★ *teens, adolescents and young adults' way as almost the only way,*
- ★ *parents and their grown up children with no common way or no way.*

Educational failure as a Socializing process is partially due to some parents deep rooted conviction that their way has to always be the only way.

Yes, parents may have more exposures and experiences. Parents may have more resources, including financial resources, than their still teens and adolescents children.

Parents' way as almost the only way has been, to some degree, traditionally the only way. And there were no major educational issues. Indeed, traditional parents, beyond their own moral authority, were guiding their children by and through divine/spiritual authority...

According to Carl G. Jung, only when our religious symbols cease to be "alive" can our psyche be looked upon objectively.

Men from the medical profession were the first to observe our psyche. Psychology emerged directly from the sickness and spiritual uneasiness of modern man.

When we fail our children' education, it doesn't matter what other success they achieve in life such as their deep knowledge, vast practical skills, power position, name, fame, fortune, cheerful fans...they still may feel the ineffable and unbearable *Pain* of *Inner Emptiness.*

Once teens, adolescents and young adults feel the possible *Pain of Inner Emptiness,* no one and nothing material can help them alleviate it as proven by John's following sad story.

Their Own Story: In her book entitled *CHOICES,* Andrea J. Moises tells a story of a successful business man named John.

Though successful on the outside, John was deeply in trouble on the inside. He worked hard. He built a successful computer business. He made millions of dollars every year. But John felt abused by his own father who used to criticize him.

Hopeless and helpless, John internalized his anger and bitterness. He felt abused and awful about himself and life itself despite his own success.

He thought that his success in business would compensate for his inner life inadequacy. After his father's long abuse, John came to believe that he was not worthy of love. He believes that he did not deserve love and kind treatment.

He was desperate to feel good about himself but he did not know how. After work in his business, he felt awkward and unlovable. He did realize that there is life after work. He did realize that he has other deep needs along with his success in business.

John's romantic relationship never lasts long. He had nothing to give emotionally. His feeling of unworthiness fueled his need for more and more success in his business. The more time, energy and resource he gave to his business for success, the less he had left for his next girlfriend.

Depth psychologists tell us that modern man is passing through a deep crisis, especially from his deepest belief systems. Modern man's present consciousness is often said to be *a vacuum.*

Modern man is "in search of a soul." He is in search of the meaning of life. He is also in search of the meaning of his own life.

But according to Jung, the meaning modern man is looking for can be only founded, experienced, enjoyed and shared from within himself, *prior* to his own consciousness, on a base of:

* ★ *a more fundamental religious belief system,*
* ★ *a more spiritually way of being rather than the intellectual one.*

Only the emergence of new and better ways of life experienced deeply and lived meaningfully can help modern man find his soul or the meaning of life and the meaning of his own life.

If he fails it, it doesn't matter what else he finds in life, he will be heading to what neurologist, psychiatrist and logo-therapist, Viktor Emil Frankl, calls:

* ★ *the existential vacuum,*
* ★ *the existential frustration,*
* ★ *the frustrated will to meaning, to power, to money, to pleasure.*

CHAPTER 8

Treasure Every Child's Inner Treasure

*The remedy of the tragedies of life is to get away
from any intellectual categories. It is to return to
the vital immediacies of reality, of experience,
of inwardness, the truth of subjectivity...
There is salvation only in one thing, in becoming
a single individual...*

(Sorenson Kierkegaard, theologian)

Dear Teens...Be the very Captains
of your own Destiny

Of all the fields of studies and of all life unsolved mysteries,
None has as many opportunities as the study
Of man's powerful but too often untapped inner potential.
Of all the fields of life studies and of
all life unsolved mysteries,
None is as neglected as the study
Of man's powerful but too often untapped inner potential.

Dear teens, adolescents and young adults,
Cast out sporadically your net inwardly,
Identify your own true identity,
Be true to your own true identity,
Become who truly you are meant to be.
Your true identity is one of your life greatest discoveries,
Dig it deep from the inside out,
Dig it from the subtlest strings of your innermost being,
Awaken the positive side of the sleeping
giant in you that is in no other,
Treasure the priceless inner treasure in you that is in no other,
Sing out loud your life most favorite love song that is in no other,
Saw your seeds where they are the most in need,
Your day-to-day life most demanding war,
Your day-to-day life most rewarding war
Is the very war
Between you and your own true *Self.*

We can fool the whole world...and get
pats in the backs as we pass.
But our final reward will be heartaches and tears
if we have cheated on the guy in the glass.
(Dale Wimbraw, poet)

Dear parents and community leaders, the second most powerful life giving and life animating power of All For Excellence In Education or the eighth Vital but too often missing Step to every normal Child's Inner Splendor is Inner Freedom, Inner Peace, Inner Autonomy, Self-navigation...

In order to love truly, live fully alive, forgive, forget, heal, be whole, enjoy and share *Ultimate Meaning* or *Meaning as Divine Design*, open-minded teens, adolescents and young adults must know why and how to:

* *achieve in-depth self-discovery, one of their lifelong greatest discoveries,*
* *be true to their own true identity,*
* *become who truly they are meant to be.*

Open-minded teens, adolescents and young adults must know why and how to welcome the emergence of their own true *Self* by and through:

* their own in-depth self-discovery,
* their true identity,
* their inner purity, inner peace, inner autonomy, self-navigation...

The true *Self* involves but encompasses, by far:

* *the socially induced self,*
* *the self-imposed self,*
* *the dialogical encounter induced self.*

The emergence of their true *Self* is a lifelong dynamic process. Children' true *Self* sharpens their visions, deepens their worldviews and widens their horizons.

The emergence of their true *Self* is one of their smoothest roads to:

* *the Larger than Life deep within everyone of them,*
* *the Larger than Life all around everyone of them,*
* *the Larger than Life in between the best there is within and around them.*

Their true *Self* is one of their best ways to wisdom. Wisdom is part of what they need first if they are to know why and how to:

* *bring the whole world near to their heart and soul and spirit,*
* *make the whole world dear to their heart and soul and spirit,*
* *make the whole world home to their heart and soul and spirit.*

The true *Self* is virtually available and accessible to anyone at anytime and under almost any life circumstance providing that one knows why and how to enjoy and share:

★   *their healthy and free and fully alive innocent Inner Child,*
    ★   *their true and long lasting Inner Peace,*
    ★   *their healthy self-love, spiritual love and unconditional love.*

The emergence of teens, adolescents and young adults' true *Self* is vital to their true and long lasting:

    ★   *Inner Peace,*
    ★   *Peace with one another,*
    ★   *Peace within and across different cultures.*

The emergence of the true *Self* is a lifelong dynamic process. Teens, adolescents and young adults' true Self is always in the making and always in becoming. It is vital to young people's will, skills and wisdom to know why and how to:

    ★   *love truly and live fully alive,*
    ★   *forgive, forget, heal and be whole,*
    ★   *enjoy and share a meaningful life, a peaceful life, a purposeful life.*

The true *Self* is vital to teens, adolescents and young adults' ongoing struggle for *Oneness* with full *Self-awareness:*

    ★   *oneness with their loved ones and important others,*
    ★   *oneness between their knowledge/skills and innate talent,*
    ★   *oneness between what they have to do and what they are called to do,*
    ★   *oneness with the One within and all around everyone of them.*

The emergence of their own true Self is a true measure of teens, adolescents and young adults' Excellence In Education.

Become who you are, says the old saying.

Open-minded teens, adolescents and young adults need to know why and how to be true to their own true *Self* if they are to know why and how to:

- *identify what they want most out of their life,*
- *identify what they are most good at,*
- *re-align what they want the most to what they are most good at.*

Every open-minded teen, adolescent and young adult need to be fully aware and deeply convinced that:

- *there has never been someone else exactly like them,*
- *there will never be someone else exactly like them,*
- *they each are, to some degree, unique.*

All normal human beings, are each are made to make a difference:

- *in their own life,*
- *in the lives of their loved ones and important others,*
- *in the life of everyone else, including their hurtful friends and foes.*

However, the emergence of the true *Self* requires everyone to know how to:

* *love truly, live fully alive...*
* *forgive, forget, heal, be whole...*
* *enjoy and share inner peace, inner autonomy, ultimate meaning...*

I may have opponents but I do not have enemies,
I am a citizen of every thinking soul,
Truth, that's my country.
(Alfred de Lamartine, French romantic poet)

The Problem

The major barriers to the emergence of the true *Self* are the ongoing *Conflicts* between the natural and normal pairs of people' personal inner *Opposites such as*:

* *their Consciousness and their Unconscious,*
* *their Ego and their Shadow,*
* *their Persona-mask and their true and total Personality.*

The Solution

The *Harmony* between young people's natural and normal and necessary pairs of personal inner *Opposites* is the *Solution* to the ongoing *Conflict* between:

* *their Consciousness and their Unconscious,*

* *their Ego and their Shadow,*
* *their Persona-mask and their true and total Personality.*

The tension between the natural and normal pairs of youth's personal inner *Opposites* determines the intensity and abundance of their psychic energies.

The *Balance* between teens, adolescents and young adults' natural and normal pairs of personal inner *Opposites* is the too often untold *Secret* of:

* *their mental stability,*
* *their emotional balance,*
* *their healthy growth.*

If young adults are to enjoy and share the emergence of their own true *Self,* they need to know why and how to:

* *love truly and live fully alive,*
* *forgive, forget, heal and be whole,*
* *enjoy a meaningful life, a peaceful life, a purposeful life...*

The world great religious and spiritual traditions and collective wisdom tell us about the powerful life giving and life animating power of:

* *the true Self,*
* *the transcendent Self,*
* *the infinite Self.*

The Problem

The emergence of teens, adolescents and young adults' true *Self* requires:

- ★ *their true and unconditional love,*
- ★ *their strong belief systems,*
- ★ *their solid worldviews, shared values, time tested ways of life...*

The Solution

The emergence of youth's true *Self* is an ever increasing and a never ending striving for *Oneness* with full *Self-awareness:*

- ★ *oneness with their loved ones and important others,*
- ★ *oneness with the best there is within and all around them,*
- ★ *oneness with the Larger than Life within and all around them.*

All open-minded teens, adolescents and young adults are meant to meet and melt down and be *One with:*

- ★ *their own true Self,*
- ★ *one another's true Self,*
- ★ *almost everyone else's true Self.*

Young people's struggle and success to be true to their own true *Self* is one of their lifelong greatest achievements. Striving to become who truly they are meant to be is one of their lifelong smoothest roads to their true and long lasting *Fulfillment.*

Open-minded teens, adolescents and young adults' ability to identify their own true identity and to be true to their own true identity and to become who truly they are meant to be, is a pathway to:

* *their own uniqueness,*
* *their own natural gift,*
* *their own dominant talent.*

The Problem

The emergence of the true *Self is often* limited by the too limiting and misleading:

* *socially induced self,*
* *self-imposed self,*
* *dialogical encounter induced self.*

The socially induced self, the self-imposed self and the dialogical encounter induced self may often expose certain children to what psychologist, Otto Rank, and depth psychologist and psychoanalyst, Carl G. Jung, call:

* *the Fear of Life,*
* *the Fear of Death,*
* *the Empty Center.*

The Fear of Life may expose certain children to:

* *blind conformity,*

* *mediocrity,*
* *co-dependence.*

The Fear of Death may expose certain children to:

* *see their own way as the only way,*
* *aggressiveness,*
* *violence and guilty feelings.*

The *Empty Center* leaves certain children with no other alternative questions but:

* *does it work?*
* *what is in it for me?*
* *how can I get the best and the most out of it?*

The Solution

To prevent or confront and overcome *the Fear of Life, the Fear of Death and the Empty Center,* parents and other educators need to inspire all open-minded teens, adolescents and young adults to know why and how to act, interact and react, ideally at the same time, as:

* *social human beings with a deep educational need for Belonging,*
* *individual human beings with a deep educational need for Independence,*
* *socio-human beings with a deep educational need for Dialogue.*

Open-minded teens, adolescents and young adults must be aware that their loved ones and important others have their own *Expectations, Demands and Requirements.*

Parents and important others' educational Demands and Requirements may often be in Conflict with their own children's second deepest educational need for relative Independence.

As individual human beings with their second deepest and equally important educational need for relative Independence, open-minded teens, adolescents and young adults must know why and how to accept, respect and protect:

★ their own *personal Inclination,*
★ *their own Innate dominant talent,*
★ *their own big dreams, visions and life purposes.*

As social and individual human beings, open-minded teens, adolescents and young adults must know why and how to:

★ establish a two-way learning road between Belonging and Independence,
★ learn at the same time from their two first deepest educational needs,
★ enjoy and share their third deepest educational need for *Dialogue.*

On Their Own Words: According to Carl G. Jung:

* our individual life involves a flow of our psychic energy out into the world.
* our flow of psychic energy takes place through our social symbols.
* our symbols are universal in their psychological nature.
* our symbols are social in their particular historical manifestation.
* our social symbols are channels for our psychic energies into society.

CHAPTER 9

Share Mindful Culture Production

A true friend knows your weaknesses but shows your strengths; feels your fears but fortify your faith; sees your anxieties but frees your spirit; recognizes your disabilities but emphasizes your possibilities.
(William Allen Ward, author)

Dear Teens...Transcend the Matter/Spirit/Split

The third most powerful life giving and life animating power
Of *All For Excellence In Education* or the *ninth Vital Step*
To every normal *Child's Inner Splendor*
is *Mindful Culture Production.*
You live, at the same time, in a material
world and in a spiritual world,
When you try to live as if your whole
world were merely material,
You undermine and compromise your opportunity
To be in touch with and deeply touched
by the *Larger than Life:*

★ *deep within you,*
★ *all around you,*
★ *in between the best there is within you and all around you.*

Dear teens, adolescents and young adults,
You have no holistic healing without wholeness,
You have no wholeness without forgiveness,
You have no forgiveness without true love,
You have no true love without *Inner Peace,*
You have no *Inner Peace* without *Inner Purity,*
You have no *Inner Purity,*
Without openness and receptivity
To the *Magic* between the best there is
Within you and all around you.

Every tree and plant in the meadow seem to be dancing.
Those with average eyes would see as fixed and still.
(Jalal Uddin Rumi, mystic poet)

Dear parents and community leaders, the third most powerful life giving and life animating power of All For Excellence In Education or the ninth Vital but too often missing Step to every normal Child's Inner Splendor is Mindful Culture Production.

The world is, at the same time, as we all see it and as we each see it. There is always some room for everyone to find new and better ways of:

* *seeing the world,*
* *being in the world,*
* *making the world a better place for someone.*

Even an innocent and loving smile given to an innocent child may be a new and a better way of:

* *seeing the world,*
* *being in the world,*
* *making the world a better place for someone.*

For the mindful observer, there is always something:

* *more,*
* *bigger,*
* *better.*

Their Own Story: Nelson Mandela: A Mindful Culture Producer

It is said that Nelson Mandela was a very private person. Privately, he lived an austere life. Privately, he went on as far as to make his own bed even when he became the President of his Country, South Africa.

Nelson Mandela was also known as a very loyal and courteous person with almost everyone including his political opponents. He is considered as the founding father of South African democracy.

For instance, Nelson Mandela said that:

"Those who conduct themselves with morality, integrity...need not fear of the forces of inhumanity and cruelty."

Within a decade after the end of his presidency, Mandela was widely thought of as "The golden age of hope and democracy" in South Africa.

His struggle against the political racial regime of Apartheid cost him 27 long-years of his life in prison. Upon his release, he became the first black President of his country, South Africa.

Mandela has earned international recognition and acclaim for his fight for the freedom for all and for racial equality and justice for all.

Mandela is viewed as a "moral authority" with a great concern for truth. In 1993, Mandela, along with South Africa President de Klerk, received the joint Nobel Peace Prize.

Mandela became a worldwide renowned and celebrated fighter for freedom for all and for racial reconciliation and equality for all.

In 2009, the United Nations General Assembly proclaimed Mandela birthday, July, 18, as "Mandela Day" for his contribution to the anti-Apartheid struggle.

"Mandela Day" calls on individuals to donate 67 minutes of their time doing something good to someone else. These 67 minutes represente symbolically the 67 years Mandela spent fighting the political racial regime of Apartheid.

Mandela was awarded the United States Presidential Medal of Freedom. He was also the first living person to be made an honorary Canadian citizen.

To some degree, there have always been people like Nelson Mandela. To some degree, there will always be some people like Nelson Mandela.

These extraordinary people know why and how to dedicate their life to a lofty purpose and a worthy cause for as many people as possible.

These people fight with all their might to know why and how to enjoy, share and celebrate true and long lasting:

- ★ *love for all even in the midst of hatred,*
- ★ *compassion for all even in the midst of racial injustice,*
- ★ *peace for all even in the midst of social inequality.*

The ultimate longing for mindful culture production is what motivated Mandela to enjoy and share:

- ★ *during his long struggle against the racial regime of Apartheid,*
- ★ *during his 27 years in prison against the racial regime of Apartheid,*
- ★ *during and after his years as the President of his country, South Africa.*

Mindful culture producers know why and how to enjoy and share the ineffable something more and bigger and better:

- ★ *deep within each and everyone of us all as a whole,*
- ★ *all around each and everyone of us all as a whole,*
- ★ *in between the best there is within and all around everyone of us all.*

Mindful culture producers fight with all their might to bring out the best there is within and all around everyone including:

- ★ *their hurtful friends and foes,*
- ★ *their political opponents,*
- ★ *their worst enemies.*

The stories and struggles of mindful culture producers such as Gandhi, Martin Luther King, Mother Teresa, Nelson Mandela...are living examples on why and how some realize their own self by and through helping others realize their own self.

For spiritual gurus and depth psychologists, we each and all are meant to make the world a better place to be for someone else: for everyone else.

All it takes us to succeed is to be fully aware and deeply convinced that we each and all are spiritually meant to:

* *love truly and live fully alive...*
* *forgive all, forget, heal, be whole....*
* *share a meaningful life in a meaningful world for all.*

We each and all are meant to fight with all our might to make the world more meaningful, more peaceful, more purposeful, more likeable and more enjoyable for someone: for everyone.

To succeed, we need to see the world by and through our loved ones and important others':

* *strong belief systems,*
* *solid worldviews,*
* *shared values and time tested ways of life.*

But to become *the Mindful Culture Producers,* they each and all are meant to be, all open-minded teens, adolescents and young adults need also know why and how to:

* *read between the lines,*
* *learn how to unlearn so that they could learn better,*
* *deal more constructively with life unavoidable uncertainties...*

As American great anthropologist, Margaret Mead, said:

"Culture is all we add to nature."

As mindful culture producers, we each and all are meant to be, we each and all have all the potentialities to:

* bring the whole world near to our heart and soul and spirit,
* *make the whole world dear to our heart and soul and spirit,*
* *make the whole world home to our heart and soul and spirit.*

When healthy and free and fully alive, we each and all have all the potentialities we need to know why and how to:

* *awaken the positive side of the sleeping giant in everyone of us,*
* *treasure the priceless inner treasure buried in everyone of us,*
* *share our lifelong most favorite love song that is in no other.*

We each and all are meant to acquire all the required will and skills and wisdom we need to:

* *be the Peaceful Culture Consumers we each and all are born to be,*
* *become the Captains of our destiny we each and all are meant to be,*
* *become the Mindful Culture Producers we each and all are meant to be.*

For open-minded teens, adolescents and young adults to become the *Mindful Culture Producers* they each and all are meant to be, they need to know why and how to see:

- ★ *a message beneath every mess,*
- ★ *adversity as a great university,*
- ★ *a star beyond every scar.*

When seen with unconditional love and compassion for all, our life's greatest adversities can be, to some degree, some of our lifelong greatest universities.

Once our teens, adolescents and young adults feel wise enough to become *the Mindful Culture Producers* they are meant to be, they will realize that they each and all have all the potentialities to:

- ★ *read between the lines,*
- ★ *learn how to unlearn,*
- ★ *see more than the eye can see.*

The problem

There are 3 major barriers to *Mindful Culture Production,* that is:

- ★ *all reason and no emotion,*
- ★ *all logic and no intuition,*
- ★ *all hard work and no smart work.*

Every man or woman you meet is made of reason and emotion.

Our reason is about our conscious attitudes or Persona-mask.

Our emotions are part of our true and total *Personality*, including the dark and ugly and repressed and rejected side of our *Personal Unconscious*.

Mindful Culture Production is possible anytime and anywhere. It may be available to anyone at any time and under almost any life circumstance. All it requires is true and long lasting deep longing for:

* *inner freedom and freedom of speech for all,*
* *inner peace, inner autonomy, self-navigation for all,*
* *openness and receptivity to subjectivity, originality, naivety, creativity...*

To become *the Mindful Culture Producers* they are meant to be, grown up children should know why and how to:

* *identify their own true identity,*
* *be true to their own true identity,*
* *become who truly they are meant to be.*

Our children' openness and receptivity to who truly they are precedes and prepares their openness and receptivity to:

* *what they want most out of their life,*
* *what they are most good at,*
* *the magic between what they have and are called to do.*

On Their own Words: Japanese philosopher, Kakuzo Okakura, said that:

One day Soshy was walking on the bank of a river with a friend. "How delightfully," exclaimed Soshy "are the fishes enjoying themselves in the river."

"You are not a fish, how do you know that the fishes are enjoying themselves?" objected Soshy's friend.

"You are not myself," said Soshy, "how do you know that I do not know that the fishes are enjoying themselve?" (re-adapted from Ellen J. Langer, Ph.D. "The Power of MINDFUL Learning," 1977)

Highly creative people:

* ★ *identify a domaine they love,*
* ★ *choose a field where they have the potentiality to excel,*
* ★ *re-align their hard work to their smart work.*

Mindful Culture Producers are open and receptive to almost everything but they are attached to almost nothing.

Mindful Culture Producers know why and how to learn from everything. They know why and how to learn from their life's biggest mistakes. They know how to learn from their life's greatest adversities.

Mindful Culture Producers' in depth self-discovery is their pathway to:

* the knowledge and skills relevant to their innate talent,
* the the magic between what they have to do and are called to do,
* their profession relevant to their vocation.

Excellence in their Education is what helps teens, adolescents and young adults to know why and how to:

* endure and overcome many of their life's unavoidable Conflicts,
* welcome the emergence of their own true Self,
* make the world a better place for someone staring by their own Self.

As French poet, Victor Hugo said:
When I am talking about myself,
I am talking about you,
Shame on those who think that I am not you.

At a certain level, the deepest and/or the highest level, we each and all can be seen, to some degree, as the same important members of the same important family: the Human Family.

But there cannot be *Mindful Culture Production* when there is no:

* true and long lasting Inner Peace...
* true and unconditional love, forgiveness, healing, wholeness...
* a meaningful, peaceful, purposeful life...

The Solution

Like Nelson Mandela, and many other known and unknown heroes all over the world, to be a *Mindful Culture Producer* is to know why and how to:

* ★ *love truly and live fully alive...*
* ★ *help as many as possible to bring out their own best...*
* ★ *share a meaningful and a peaceful life in a meaningful world.*

On Their own words: In her book, *The Power Of Mindful Learning,* Harvard University professor of psychology, Ellen L. Langer, said that:

We can change school curricula, change standards for testing students and teachers, increase parents and community involvement in the process of education, and increase the budget for education so that more students can become part of the computer age/ None of these measures alone will make enough difference unless students are given the opportunity to learn more mindfully...

Whether the learning takes places---in school, on the job, in the home--- whether the learning is particularly theoretical, personal or interpersonal, whether it it involves abstract concepts, such as physics, or concrete skills, such as how to play a sport, the way the information is learned will determine how, why, and when it is used.

According to the world famous psychiatrist, depth psychologist and psychoanalyst, Carl G. Jung, our society continues to function effectively only if it provides meaning to the individual persons by and through their faith and/or spiritually ways of being.

Only then can our personal psychic energies can move smoothly directly into the external world toward a socially productive life required by the community.

Our culture has to provide us with meaningful living symbols otherwise, the individual persons turn into themselves in search for new meaning.

If our psychic energy continues to regress and goes deeper and deeper into the deepest layers of the psyche, the adaptation we want to make as individuals may involve more than the outer and too often superficial world.

It may involve our longing for *Harmony* within the psyche. The transfer of the psychological problem goes from the outer world to the inner world. The key problem of our individuality is not an adaptation to the external life, but in finding the meaning of life itself.

CONCLUSION

Dear parents and community leaders, *All For Excellence In Education (AFEIE)* is vital *to Inner Peace, Inner Autonomy, Peace* with one another, Social Harmony and Peace within and across all cultures.

The world great religious and spiritual traditions and collective wisdom tell us that:

* *we each and all are created at God image,*
* *we each and all are created at God likeness,*
* *God is all loving, all knowing, all powerful.*

That means that we each and all are divinely and spiritually meant to be:

* *all loving,*
* *all knowing,*
* *all powerful.*

But the day-to-life unavoidable *Conflicts,* the natural and normal ongoing personal inner *Opposites* and the possible fears, failures, lacks and temporary setbacks are also telling us that we each and all are merely:

* *what we know,*
* *what we do,*

★ *what we have.*

The larger the gap between who we are divinely and spiritually meant to be and who we happen to be in our day-to-day life, the deeper and more unfathomable our possible *Inner Void.*

Our deep and unfathomable possible Inner Void is at the root cause of the ineffable and unbearable possible *Pain of Inner Emptiness.*

Our teens, adolescents and young adults exposures to their deeply wounded innocent Inner Child, to their deep and unfathomable possible Inner Void and to their ineffable and unbearable possible Pain of Inner Emptiness may often drag them into the bottomless abyss of what neurologist and logo-therapist, Viktor E. Frankl, calls:

★ *the existential vacuum,*
★ *the existential frustration,*
★ *the frustrated will to meaning, to power, to money and to pleasure.*

Dear parents and community leaders, our open-minded teens, adolescents and young adults need to know that they live, at the same time, in a material world and in a spiritual world.

Therefore, one of their lifelong first and most costly mistakes is to try to live as if their whole world were merely material. That is why and how certain teens, adolescents and young adults undermine and compromise their openness and receptivity to:

*   *divine/spiritual love, healthy self-love, unconditional love...*
*   *ultimate meaning or super-meaning or meaning as divine design,*
*   *a meaningful life in a more meaningful world for every thinking soul.*

We each and all are divinely meant to act and interact and react, at the same time, as:

*   *social human beings,*
*   *individual human beings,*
*   *spiritual beings.*

As social human beings, teens, adolescents and young adults are, to some degree, what their loved ones and important others want them to be. They each and all are inherently social beings in nature.

They cannot survive and thrive without love, caring and support from their loved ones and important others.

But as individual human beings, teens, adolescents and young adults will also only be, to some degree, what they make their own self to be. Therefore they need to know why and how to be the very captains of their own destiny.

They must know why and how to work, at the same time, hard and smart to:

*   *awaken the positive side of their own inner splendor that is in no other,*

★   *treasure their own priceless inner treasure that in no other,*

    ★   *share their life's most favorite love song that has never been sung before.*

As spiritual beings, teens, adolescents and young adults need to be fully aware that they each and all are divinely/spiritually meant to transcend their natural and normal but too often limiting and misleading socially induced self, self-imposed self and dialogue induced self.

They each and all need to be fully aware and deeply convinced that they are divinely, spiritually and psychologically meant to be:

    ★   *one with their own true, transcendent, infinite Self,*

    ★   *one with one another's true, transcendent, infinite Self,*

    ★   *one with almost everyone else's true, transcendent, infinite Self.*

ABOUT THE AUTHOR

Malick Kouyate holds a Doctoral Degree in Education from the University of Pittsburgh (1999), a Masters Degree in Public Policies and Management (MPM) from Carnegie Mellon University (1995) and a Bachelor Degree in Philosophy from the University of Conakry, Guinea.

After 40 years of professional experiences in Education, Dr. Kouyate is a well known educational scholar, philosopher, poet, inspirational writer and a motivational speaker. He is the author of *How To Educate All For Excellence (Trafford Publishing, 2013)* and the co-founder of *All For Excellence In Education (AFEIE)*.

Dr. Kouyate believes that to *Educate All For Excellence* is to inspire all children in general and all open-minded teens, adolescent and young adults in particular to know *why* and *how* to enjoy and share their 4 deepest educational needs for *Belonging, for relative Independence, for Dialogical Encounter* and for *Self-navigation*.

Dr. Kouyate's mission in life is to inspire life learning and life changing experiences relevant to *healthy self-love, spiritual love, unconditional love, forgiveness, healing, wholeness, ultimate meaning, inner peace, peace with one another within and across different cultures.*

He believes that true and long lasting love for all, including for our hurtful friends and foes, is our smoothest road to *a more meaningful and peaceful life in a more meaningful and peaceful world for every thinking soul.*

To schedule consultations, conferences, seminars, webinars, workshops...please contact:

Dr. Malick Kouyate or Aissata Diallo at: (412) 621-1344 or (412) 478-4670
Malick.kouyate53@gmail.com or Aissatadiallo74@gmail.com

REFERENCES

Allen N. Mendler: *Motivating Students Who Don't Care: Successful Techniques For Education.* Solution Tree, Bloomington, Indiana, 2000.

Astra Taylor: *Examined Life*: *Excursion With Contemporary Thinkers.* The New York Press; 2009.

Charles I. Glicksberg: *The Self In Modern Literature.* The Pennsylvania State University Press, Park University, PA, 1963.

Cynthia Kersey: *Unstoppable: 45 Powerful Stories of Perseveration and Triumph from People Like You.* Couserbook Inc., Naperville, Illinois, 1998.

Dennis P. Kimbro: *What Makes The Great, Great: Strategies For Extraordinary Achievement.* Doubleday, New York, N.Y, 1998.

Dick De Vos: *Rediscovering American Values: The Foundation Of Our Freedom For the 21ˢᵗ Century.* Penguin Group, New York, 1997.

Edward Osers: *The Meaning of Hitler: Hitler's Use of Power: His Success and Failures.* Translated by Sabastian Haffner, Macmillan Publishing C O, Inc., New York, NY, 1979.

Eckhart Tolle: *The Power of Now: A Guide To Spiritual Enlightenment.* Namaste Publishing, Vancouver, Canada, 1999.

Eckhart Tolle: *A New Earth: An Awakening To Your Life Purpose.* A Plume Book, 2005.

Ellen J. Langer: *The Power of Mindful Learning.* A Merloyd Lawrence Book, Massachusetts, 1987.

Ellen J. Langer: *Mindfulness.* A Merloyd Lawrence Book. Massachusetts, 1989.

Flowers, Steve & Stahl, Bob: *Living Your Heart Wide Open: How Mindfulness Can Free You From Unworthiness, Inadequacy & Shame.* New Harbinger Publishing, Inc., CA,2011.

Ferrari, M.,& Sternberg, Robert.,: *Self-awareness: Its Nature and Development.* The Guilford

Freire P.: *Teachers as Cultural Workers: Letters of Those who Dare to Teach.* West-view Press, 1999.

Fromm Erich: *To Have or To Be?* Harper and Row, Publishers, 1976.

Gary Chapman: *Love As A Way Of Life: 7 Keys To Transforming Every Aspect Of Your Life.* Doubleday, New York, 2008.

Gerald L. Gutek: *American Education 1945-2000: A History and Commentary.* Waveland Press. Inc., Long Grove, Illinois, 2000.

Kahlil Gibran: *The Prophet.* Afred Kno

Kenneth P. Kramer: *Martin Buber's Spirituality: Hasidic Wisdom For Everyday Life.* New Yo**rk,** 1923.

Gloria Steinem: *A Revolution From Within: A Book of Self-esteem.* Little, Brown and Company, 1992-1993.. Rowman & Littlefield Publishers, Maryland, 1994.

Helen Palmer: *Inner Knowing: Consciousness, Creativity, Insight and Intuition.* Jeremy P.Tarcher, New York, 1997.

Ira Progoff: *Jung's Psychology and its Social Meaning.* Groove Press and Evergreen Books 64, University Place, New York, N.y, 1953.

James Garbarino: *Lost Boys: Why Our Sons Turn Violents and How We Can Help Them.* The Free Press, New York, NY 10020, 1999.

Jeremiah Abrams: *Reclaiming The Inner Child.* Jeremy P. Tarcher, Inc., Los Angeles, 1999.

John Edward: *Infinite Quest: Develop Your Psychic Intuition To Change Your Life.* Sterling Publishing, New York, 2008.

Johnahan, Star: *The Inner Treasure: An Introduction To the World's Sacred and Mystical Writings.* Jeremy P. Tarcher/ Putman, New York, N.Y, 1999.

Joshua L. Liebman: *Peace of Mind.* Simon & Schuster, New York, 1946.

John P. Schuster: *Answering Your Calling: A Guide For Living Your Deepest Purpose.* Berret-Choehler Publishers, Inc., San Francisco, 2003.

Johnston, William: *The Inner Eye Of Love: Mysticism and Religion.* Fordham University Press, New York, 1997.

Life Books: *100 People Who Change The World.* Volume 10, No 3; May 28, 2010.

Leonard, George: *The Silent Pulse: A Search For The Perfect Rhythm That Exists In Each One Of Us.* Gibbs Smith, Publisher, Utah, 2006.

Lewis M. Andrews: *To Thin Own Self Be True: The Relationship Between Spiritual Values And Emotional Health.* Doubleday Dell Publishing Group, Inc., New York, 1987, 1989.

Mihaley Csihszentmihaleyi: *Flow: The Psychology Of Optimal Experience:* Harpers & Row Publishers, New York, 1990.

Malick Kouyate: *Trust As Component Of The Accountability System In The Academic Standard System.* Doctoral Dissertation, University Of Pittsburgh, PA, 1999.

Malick Kouyate: *Love: The Young Adult Road To A More Meaningful Life.* Booksurge, 2009.

Malick Kouyate: *How To Educate All For Excellence: Excellent learners' 7 Deepest Educational Needs.*Trafford Publishing, 2013.

Malick Kouyate: *Dear Parent: Listen To Your Teens' Unheard Cry for True Love, Meaning and Success.* Trafford Publishing, 2014.

Mike Huckabee: *Kids Who Kill: Are We Reaping What We've Sown?* Broadman and Holman Publishers, Nashville, Tennessee, 1998.

Murray Stein: *Jung's Map of The Soul: An Introduction.* Open Court Publishing. Chicago and La Salle, Illinois. 1998.

Os Guinness: *Long Journey HOME: A Guide To Your Search For Meaningful Life.* Water Brook Press & Doubleday, 2001.

Osche, R: *The Gate Of Excellence: The Determinant of Creative Genius,* University Press, 1990.

Ralph W. Emerson: *Essay and Lectures.* University of Cambridge Press. UK, 1984.

Ralph W. Trine: *In Tune With The Infinite*. Jeremy Tarcher/ Penguin Edition, 2008.

Roman Espejo: *Violent Children*. Greenhaven Press, Fammington, MI, 2010.

Rumi J. Udin: *The Soul Of Rumi*. Translated by C. Barks. Harper Collins, San Francisco, 2002.

Seth Kreisberg: *Transforming Power: Dominion, Empowerment, Education*. State University of New York Press, New York, 1992.

Tom Morris: *True Success: A New Philosophy Of Excellence: A Joyful Approach To Work, Love and Play That Restore The Missing Ingredient In Life*. The Berkley Publishing Group, New York, 1991.

Viktor E. Frankl: *The Unheard Cry For Meaning: Psychotherapy and Humanism*. Simon and Schuster, New York, NY, 1978.

Viktor E. Frankl: *Man Search For Meaning*. Boston, Beacon Press, Boston, Massachusetts, 2006.

Wayne Tesdale: *The Mystic Heart: Discovering A Universal Spirituality In The World's Religions*. New World Library, Novoto, CA, 1999.